Screw Work,
Let's Play

Screw Work, Let's Play

How to do what you love and get paid for it

JOHN WILLIAMS

**Prentice Hall
Business
is an imprint of**

Harlow, England • London • New York • Boston • San Francisco • Toronto • Sydney • Singapore • Hong Kong
Tokyo • Seoul • Taipei • New Delhi • Cape Town • Madrid • Mexico City • Amsterdam • Munich • Paris • Milan

PEARSON EDUCATION LIMITED

Edinburgh Gate
Harlow CM20 2JE
Tel: +44 (0)1279 623623
Fax: +44 (0)1279 431059
Website: www.pearsoned.co.uk

First published in Great Britain in 2010

Pearson Education is not responsible for the content of third party internet sites.

ISBN: 978-0-273-73093-4

British Library Cataloguing-in-Publication Data
A catalogue record for this book is available from the British Library

Library of Congress Cataloguing-in-Publication Data
Williams, John, 1965-
  Screw work, lets play : how to do what you love and get paid for it / John Williams.
      p. cm.
  ISBN 978-0-273-73093-4 (pbk.)
 1. Job satisfaction. 2. Vocational guidance. 3. Career development. 4. Success.
I. Title.
  HF5549.5.J63.W55 2010
  650.1--dc22

10 9 8 7 6 5 4 3 2
14 13 12 10

Typeset in 10pt Photina by 30
Printed and bound in Great Britain by Henry Ling Limited, at the Dorset Press, Dorchester, DT1 1HD

To my father,
Edward Glyn Williams
for five months of play

Contents

About this book

This book will show you step by step how to get paid to play by turning the things you most love doing into a living. Whether you're currently feeling trapped in a job you don't enjoy or you're slogging away at your own business that's never quite taken off, you'll find both the life-changing concepts and the practical strategies you need to transform your working life.

This is not about just having fun and hoping the money will magically fall out of the sky. I will show you the key to getting paid for doing what feels like play to you, how to win your first 'playcheque', and then how to scale it up to making a living – and maybe even get rich. And if you still have no idea what you want to do with your life, I'll show you how to get clear on that first.

Whether you want to launch your own business or freelance career, create your ideal job from scratch, write a book, get famous for your art, or change the world, this book will help you. I can't show you how to 'get rich quick'. I haven't found anything yet that does that (let me know if you do!). If anything, it's about how to get *happy* quick. The fact is, whatever you want your life to be, you can create some taste of your ideal right now in the present. Doing this will make you happier and, as you will see, happiness often leads to success and wealth.

The ten secrets

The book is arranged as ten secrets to getting paid to play. These are not secrets that anyone is wilfully withholding from you and yet it's remarkable how few of us know them. We're certainly not taught them in school or college. They sometimes run counter to commonly held wisdom we hear every day and, until you know them, you are likely to be trapped forever in unsatisfying work.

The secrets are arranged in sequence to take you all the way from having no idea what work you would enjoy to making a full-time living doing something you love. It's therefore best to read each chapter in sequence as each one builds on the last.

This is what you will discover in each chapter.

Secret one: How to work out what you really really want

If you know you want to do something different but can't for the life of you work out what it is, this will finally help you. And if you're already on the way to doing what you want, don't skip this chapter because it will show just how important choosing the right work is to becoming a success.

Secret two: How to choose what to do next

How to find the sweet spot between what you love doing and what people will pay for. How to choose what avenue to pursue even when you feel completely stuck – either because you have no idea what you want or because you have so many ideas you can't make up your mind. Oh, and the scientifically proven formula for happiness.

Secret three: How to get started right now

How to escape the trap of endless research and get started right away on your new life. Why you don't need elaborate plans or even to set goals. How to start even the grandest project in a scaled-down form without quitting your current work.

Secret four: How to guarantee your success

It can be a rocky ride on the way to getting paid to play. Read this chapter to find out how you can become indestructible and guarantee you can make it whatever may happen along the way.

Secret five: How to play for profit

Worried that doing what you really enjoy will land you in poverty? This chapter will show you how to do things that are fun for you in a way that provides real value to people – and so get paid for it.

Secret six: How to play the fame game – and win

How to get known, or even famous, for what you do so that you attract the opportunities you want. How to start using the latest online social media systems to help you launch yourself onto the world at little or no cost.

Secret seven: How to create an irresistible offer

How to offer something people really want and choose the best way to deliver it, from selling a service to creating something on the internet that makes you money while you sleep.

Secret eight: How to win your first playcheque

How to earn your very first piece of income for something that feels like play to you – without having to quit your current work.

Secret nine: How to play full time

How to scale up your first experiments to something you can get paid for full time whether in self-employment, a portfolio career, or in what I call Job 2.0 – the customised job. How to make it happen quicker than you might expect.

Secret ten: How to play your way to the rich life

This chapter will show you how to get clear what a rich life looks like to you; is it financial riches, the freedom to travel the planet, having plenty of free time, or the power to change the world? Discover the 5 keys to get you there including the P.R.I.C.E. strategy to charge what you're really worth.

The 21 myths of work

I've worked with hundreds of clients over the past five years, and over and over again I see the same mistaken beliefs that stop people from doing what they want. These are often beliefs inherited from a previous generation that had far fewer choices about their work than we do now. I've boiled these down to 21 myths. You'll find them peppered throughout the book and can see each one being dismantled. You can also read the full list at the end of the book. How many of them are you currently holding as the truth? They may well be what's holding you back. Are you ready to open your mind to some new ideas about work?

I think of the 21 myths like this: imagine an old prop plane sitting on the runway with its engine running. If you release the brakes and remove the chocks, it's inevitable that it's going to start rolling – but you're still going to need to apply some gas in order to take off. If I can just take away all the myths you believe about work, it is inevitable you will start moving towards what you want. Of course, you'll still need to apply some gas to take flight and get where you want to go.

Expert interviews

To support the ideas contained in the book, I interviewed ten successful players and quizzed them on the beliefs, habits and actions they used to get where they are. Some of them have created, run and sold million-pound businesses. But I didn't just interview the well established; I interviewed people just starting out who had a very playful approach and were already seeing some success from it. Some interviewees are very wealthy; others are living on a relatively modest income but have succeeded in structuring their lives around freedom, creativity and variety. Some are on a mission to change the world. They are all living rich lives in the broadest sense of the word.

You can read and, in some cases, listen to or watch the full interviews with the players at ScrewWorkLetsPlay.com.

The website

Throughout the book and at the end of each chapter, I have point-
ed you to further information, tools and resources on the accompanying website ScrewWorkLetsPlay.com. Go there now to listen
to audio recordings, download worksheets and read updates to
the book as they become available.

Acknowledgements

Nothing of any significance has ever been created by one person and this book is no exception. Firstly I'd like to thank Samantha Jackson at Pearson for her passion for the subject of play and for giving me a chance to share mine – and for helping to craft my ideas into the best possible shape. Thanks also to my agent and friend Jacqueline Burns of Free Agents for not only being a great agent but also going beyond the call of duty to help me develop the book. It's time to celebrate the completion of this play project – get your skates on girl, we're going ice-skating!

Thanks to the coaches I was lucky enough to learn from first-hand: business coach, colleague and friend Judith Morgan who first suggested the idea of a year off; Jerry Hyde, creativity guru, who told me to write a book and, like most of his advice, I only listened to it two years later – thanks for so much inspiration over the past seven years. Thanks also to the members of Jerry's very creative men's group who have encouraged me throughout the writing process.

Thanks to Nick Williams who first taught me about information products, and Daniel Wagner for sharing his expertise on internet marketing and warmly inviting me to step up to teach a piece of his workshop. Thanks also to Suzy Greaves, Mark Forster and Barbara Winter for inspiring me and helping me work out where I was heading. Thank you in particular to Suzy Greaves and Nina Grunfeld for reading early drafts of the manuscript.

This book owes a great debt to all the great books that have inspired and educated me over the past four decades. Especially Barbara Sher whose book I first read 15 years ago and told me I was a Scanner – what a treat to attend your Scanners Retreat so many years later. This book wouldn't be the same if you hadn't led the way.

A debt also to Pat Kane for giving us the Play Ethic and for showing us there is an alternative to the tired old work ethic. And also to Seth Godin for his very human marketing genius, and Dan Pink for his fresh take on work and careers. And respect to Roger Hamilton for the creation of his remarkable Wealth Dynamics.

Richard, Selina, Cath and Neil at Careershifters gave me the opportunity to witness the struggles (and myths) of the average working man and woman in the 20 attendees at every monthly Careershifters workshop.

Thanks to my work support group members and good friends Liz Rivers and Candy Newman. Especially Candy for so much support while I was writing. And to her son Ben Dixon, a player in the making, for being such good company on our writing retreat in Cornwall. Thanks to my friends Natasha, James and Jay for all your encouragement and wisdom. To Jacqui Loran: you can now finally stop saying 'You should write a book John'. And Teresa for helping me run Scanners Night and Julian Bolt for his great wisdom on the subject of art and artists.

Lots of love to my mum Diane Williams for teaching me that play is just as important as work and who still has plenty of play projects on the go. And to my brother David for his entrepreneurial outlook and for first coaching me on how to customise a job. Thanks to my ever-playful uncle Roger Taylor who passed away during the writing of this book. And thank you to the three generations of scientists, engineers and entrepreneurs who went before me; I hope I've done you proud.

Thank you to all my clients who bravely shared the dreams and challenges of their working lives with me and also to the test pilots on the 'Screw Work, Let's Play' Summer school of 2009.

Thanks to my busy interview subjects who were kind enough to give their time in aid of this book: Tim Smit, creator of the Eden Project (and his PA Jo Gale); Leslie Scott, creator of Jenga and author of *About Jenga*; Derek Sivers, founder of CD Baby; entrepreneur, mentor and speaker Mike Southon; Nic Roope of digital agency Poke; Sam Bompas and Harry Parr of Bompas & Parr; Chris Guillebeau of The Art of Non-Conformity; editor of *The Idler*, Tom Hodgkinson; playful author Dixe Wills; Sophie Boss of Beyond Chocolate; Petra Barran of Choc Star; and Robert Chalmers and Lindsey Mountford. Thanks to Spectrum Therapy for introducing me to my top dog and so many other great ideas and practices. To Chris Wild for your enthusiasm for this book and for connecting me with the opportunity to write it.

And finally to you for reading this book. I hope you'll go out and recruit more people to the play cause.

You can contact me at ScrewWorkLetsPlay.com or follow me on Twitter as @johnsw.

Publisher's acknowledgements

The publishers are grateful to Roger Hamilton for permission to reproduce the section on Wealth Dynamics pp50–3, adapted from www.rogerhamilton-wealthdynamics.com

In some instances we have been unable to trace the owners of copyright material, and we would appreciate any information that would enable us to do so.

Join the play revolution

For the first time in the human experience, we have a chance to shape our work to suit the way we live instead of our lives to fit our work . . . We would be mad to miss the chance.

Charles Handy, management expert and author

We're lucky. We've reached a remarkable point in the history of work. Today, it's possible to make a living out of pretty much anything. Seriously; whatever you can think of, someone somewhere in the world is making a career of it.

During the course of my research for this book I've met remarkable examples like Chris Guillebeau who is travelling to every country in the world and living off the blog he writes along the way; Sam Bompas & Harry Parr who create architectural jellies and breathable cocktails; Petra Barran who travels from festival to festival selling gourmet chocolate treats in the UK's only touring choc-mobile; Sarah de Nordwall who has carved a career as a professional bard writing poetry and performing it everywhere – from a drug rehab unit to the House of Lords.

These people are part of a growing tribe around the world who are not content just to make a wage to pay the rent, but want their lives to be about something larger – creating something unique, saying something important, trying new experiences, having some fun, taking a few risks, and daring to fall flat on their faces – or win big and strike it rich. They want freedom, variety, challenge and excitement; they want to stretch themselves, and to keep evolving every day.

What we're witnessing is no less than a revolution in what work can be. The word 'job' is irrelevant; even the word 'work' seems a poor choice for the lifestyles this new tribe have crafted for themselves. Musician turned entrepreneur, Derek Sivers, who recently sold his business for $22 million says, 'This isn't work, it's play'.

Our vocabulary is out of date. Some of these people call themselves entrepreneurs or business people but the old image of someone dressed in a sober suit spouting management speak just doesn't fit. The player's uniform is just as likely to be jeans and T-Shirt or, for those working at home, pyjamas.

Even the senior figureheads of this new tribe are more playful, irreverent, informal. They're as much in it for the creative buzz as for the money. In his book *Business Stripped Bare* Richard Branson describes being asked in an interview with senior newsman Bob Schieffer why he had gone into business: 'I just stared at him. I suddenly realised I had never been interested in being "in business". And, heaven help me, I said so, adding: "I've been interested in creating things."'

Previous generations had little choice about their working lives; a job for life was standard, and the alternative of starting a business often required expensive premises, a team of staff, and huge advertising costs. The business world was littered with gatekeepers who got to choose who could come in based on background, race, gender or any other arbitrary parameter. Now, no one can stop you crafting your work life exactly as you would like it.

The internet and mobile technology have freed us all to work however, wherever, whenever we want. Old restrictive boundaries are dissolving; between local and global; employee and entrepreneur; professional and amateur; consumer and producer; home and office; work and play. Our options are now so much broader than just employee or business owner. What does all this mean? It means that there really is no reason left to suffer boring, unfulfilling work.

We no longer need to be driven by the old work ethic; we have entered the era of what author Pat Kane calls 'The Play Ethic':

> This is 'play' as the great philosophers understood it: the experience of being an active, creative and fully autonomous person. The play ethic is about having the confidence to be spontaneous, creative and empathetic across every area of your life . . . It's about placing yourself, your passions and enthusiasms at the centre of your world.
>
> **Pat Kane, author of** The Play Ethic: A Manifesto for a Different Way of Living, **taken from www.theplayethic.com**

Does 'play' sound selfish to you? It's actually the opposite. Players are often as interested in what they can give to the world as what they can get from it. Tim Smit left the music business to create 'the world's first rock 'n' roll scientific foundation' at the Eden Project. Innocent Drinks, the famously playful brand with the majority share of the UK smoothie market, have committed 10 per cent of their profits to The Innocent Foundation. They are funding projects to help some the world's poorest people in the countries where they source their fruit. And Google, famed for its playful work environment, kicked, off its not-for-profit arm with a $1 billion fund. Its mission is to address some of the world's most urgent problems including climate change, global public health, and poverty.

So are you ready to play? Perhaps you're currently stuck in a job that's reducing you to tears. Or you're slogging away at a business that's never quite taken off. In all likelihood you've been doing a lot of thinking about this, going round and round in circles trying to discover the way out. Well, it's time to end all that. Let's begin your transformation from worker to player. This book will show you the way – how to have fun and get paid for it; how to design a life big enough to hold everything that you are; how to explore and indulge your every interest; how to embrace a new world of uncertainty and enjoy the ride; how to get results you never dared dream of with a lot less struggle; and how to stop waiting and get started on all this right now.

Join the revolution

It is my opinion that the 21st century will be the century of play.

Brian Sutton-Smith, Professor Emeritus of Education at the
University of Pennsylvania and prominent play theorist

American author Daniel Pink is a leading thinker on the changing world of work. In his recent book *A Whole New Mind* he suggests we have reached a new era requiring very different skills if we want to stay in the game. Back in the nineteenth century the industrial revolution gave us massive factories and efficient assembly lines. The factory worker needed physical strength and manual skills to thrive. The twentieth century ushered in the information age with the knowledge worker who needed analytical and logical skills. Today in the twenty-first century we find ourselves in the Conceptual Age. The skills we need now, Pink says, are what you might call right-brain functions such as design, empathy, meaning and play. Those of us showing inventiveness, empathy, and big picture capabilities – players – will be the ones to excel.

This is not a shift you can sit back and opt out of. Logical Information Age skills are still necessary but they will no longer be sufficient. Work that can be easily defined and reproduced is likely to be either automated or outsourced. New forms of automation are now affecting this generation's white-collar workers in similar ways as it did last generation's blue-collar workers. To survive, you must develop skills that computers can't do better, faster, or cheaper. What can't be automated may be outsourced to equally capable but cheaper staff in other countries like India, China and the Philippines. This has already extended from IT to financial analysis, editorial work, legal research and completing tax returns.

The industrial revolution, predicated on the Protestant work ethic, gave us the *worker*. Today's digital revolution has given us the *player*.

Don't be one of those workers that use the current state of the economy as an excuse to put off making a change: people that say they're not thinking about their career right now because there's a recession on (or the recession is only just over, or they've heard there's going to be another recession . . .) so they should just keep their head down, stay put and play safe.

Burying your head in the sand is the last thing you should be doing in a time of huge change and uncertainty. Firstly, this is the time you are most likely to lose your job. If your boss calls you in this Friday and says it's your last day, wouldn't you rather have done the thinking already on what to do next than have to rush to start from scratch the following Monday? Secondly, it's in the times of greatest change that the most exciting opportunities emerge. More people became millionaires during the Great Depression than in any other time in American history.

This book will show you how to test out your new line of work without quitting what you do now so that you're ready when the recovery comes – or when you feel brave enough to jump anyway. And if you're reading this book because you've been made redundant, don't waste this chance to rethink your work and move towards play.

It pays to have fun

I never went into business to make money – but I have found that, if I have fun, the money will come.

Sir Richard Branson, founder of Virgin

Having fun is at the heart of the idea of playing. And fun makes good financial sense too. The world's richest and most successful people including billionaires Richard Branson, Steve Jobs, Warren Buffett and Oprah Winfrey say they do what they do because it's fun. They clearly don't continue working because they need the money.

Here's the advice of Steve Jobs, CEO of Apple Computer and former CEO of Pixar Animation Studios, as given at his Stanford University commencement address:

> *Your work is going to fill a large part of your life, and the only way to be truly satisfied is to do what you believe is great work. And the only way to do great work is to love what you do. If you haven't found it yet, keep looking. Don't settle.*

If you're currently chasing success and money in an attempt to make yourself happy you may have got things the wrong way round. Research by Professor Sonja Lyubomirsky of the University of California recently revealed that happiness, in many cases, leads to successful outcomes, rather than merely following from them.

After reviewing 225 relevant studies, her results show that happier people are more creative and productive, more likely to attempt new challenges, and to push themselves to strive for fresh goals. They are also more likely to be liked by their peers, and thus recruited to better jobs and promoted to higher positions. As a result of all this, happy people accrue more money.

So how do we become happier? Choosing the right work is a good start. The evidence demonstrates that people who have jobs distinguished by autonomy, meaning and variety are significantly happier than those who don't. As the good professor explains,

> *When it comes to work life, we can create our own so-called 'upward spirals.' The more successful we are at our jobs, the higher income we make, and the better work environment we have, the happier we will be. This increased happiness will foster greater success, more money, and an improved work environment, which will further enhance happiness, and so on and so on and so on.*

This book will show you how to begin this upward spiral by choosing the right work and by creating a happier, more enjoyable life in the present.

When you find yourself in love with something you're good at, you never really work again.

Sir Ken Robinson, British author and expert on creativity and education

The key to getting paid for playing is to choose the right things to play. And the right things are those that you are naturally good at. Your aim must be to get into 'flow', as serial entrepreneur Roger Hamilton calls it. Build a working life around the things you enjoy doing and have a natural talent for. But to do this, you need to widen your perception of what constitutes a talent far beyond the limited concept of 'transferable skills'.

It's important to understand the distinction between talent and skill. Talent appears early in life. Using our talents feels good so we do it a lot. Skill comes later as a result of practising that talent. We are musical before we ever pick up an instrument. People who are great communicators have usually been chatting to anyone who would listen since they formed their first words. Writers often start reading early. Great salespeople have been influencing and negotiating since they started school. Success is so much easier and more enjoyable when we build our work around our natural talents and developed skills.

So if we understand this, why aren't we all getting paid to have fun? Firstly, a lot of people are simply doing the wrong work. Most of us have made gross compromises in our choice of work, driven by the principles of a previous generation who didn't have the options we do today. We have never dared to be selective enough about what we do so that we can spend the majority of the time in flow. As a result we haven't sown that rich seam of gold among the masses of grey rock.

Some people think it's nonsense to make a living out of what you love because they've never experienced it. The school system sets us up for this when it encourages us to work on our weaknesses. Forget it. Work on your strengths, work *around* your weaknesses.

But, of course, in a conventional job it can be difficult to say 'I don't do presentations, I only do research' or 'I don't do research, I only do presentations'. We're supposed to be great all-rounders – good at being creative, organising our time, working in a team, creating thorough reports, presenting our findings, and dotting the I's and crossing the T's. In reality no one can excel at all these things, and trying to do so guarantees mediocrity. The result is that work becomes a struggle and we lose sight of just how talented we are.

When you finally work *with* your personality and strengths, and avoid the ill-fitting work that drags you down, the effect is like dropping into a jetstream. You will see not just an incremental improvement in your results but a dramatic multiplication.

This is one reason why people are increasingly attracted to various forms of self-employment.

Get the autonomy you crave

Given the limitations of conventional jobs, it's not surprising so many people would like an alternative. A survey in 2006 found that a third of all employees were seriously considering self-employment or had already taken steps to work for themselves. No doubt many more dream of doing something similar but never dare take the steps. Too many are held back by the myths of what it takes to work for yourself (we'll be dismantling every one of these myths later in the book).

A common belief is that the natural alternative to a job is to launch a business with all the risk and complexities of premises, staff and funding. But there are now so many different ways to make an income without a job: self-employed, internet marketing, passive income streams, portfolio career, micro-business. The line between employed and self-employed is blurred and it is no longer necessary to jump straight from one to another. Now we can test out our ideas, prove that they work and earn our first *playcheque* before we quit – or we can just keep it as a nice sideline to our employment. We can even reinvent the humble job to create the 'customised job', moulded to suit our personality, and our preferred working structure and location.

Whatever its form, the difference is primarily one of attitude. It's a shift in responsibility from passive employee to active creator; a 180-degree about-turn, from looking outward for someone else to define our work to looking inward and creating the working life we really want. It's the shift from worker to player.

This is a new century and it's a new world of business. The industrial revolution gave us mass production – treating employees as interchangeable components in a machine, creating generic products, and selling them to a mass market of undifferentiated consumers. Nearly two centuries later, today's digital revolution is changing the face of work all over again but this time it's about a shift towards individuals and micro-businesses creating innovative products for niche markets, and attracting fans that market the products they like to each other. Business is becoming sexy and entrepreneurship is the new rock 'n' roll.

The world will be your office

Thanks to laptop computers, mobile phones, and Wi-Fi, we are now freed from the tyranny of the office cubicle. If your work is portable, you are free to choose where you work and who with. You'll find the new free-range humans in parks, cafés and even sitting beside the swimming pool. Bored of your dreary co-workers? Now you can find your people in a loose work gathering like Jelly, a semi-weekly work-together that's taking place in over a hundred cities where people have come together in a person's home, a coffee shop, or an office to work for the day. As the Jelly site says, 'We provide chairs and sofas, wireless internet, and interesting people to talk to, collaborate with, and bounce ideas off of. You bring a laptop (or whatever you need to get your work done) and a friendly disposition.'

For a more consistent sense of community, you can become a member of one of the many shared workspaces popping up around the world that sell desk space by the hour or month. This book was largely written in a workspace for social entrepreneurs called The Hub. Now with branches in 12 cities around the world, it's a workspace, meeting space, café and social community. The members are people who want to build businesses and organisations where making a difference is as important as making a profit. Similar spaces are appearing for artists, media professionals and start-up businesses.

Once you're free of the office, the next step is to realise that you may also be free of the country you live in. Why not join the growing tribe of 'digital nomads':

Case study

Management consultant Lea Woodward and her graphic designer partner Jonathan Woodward were both working exhausting hours in corporations when they decided to do something completely different.

They launched their own businesses as a freelance graphic designer and business coach. It dawned on them that they could run their businesses from anywhere in the world and enjoy a higher standard of living for the same or lower cost. So after six months, they decided to leave the UK to find somewhere new to make their home.

Now, after two years on the road, Lea and Jonathan have run their businesses from Panama, Buenos Aires, Grenada, Toronto, Grenada, Dubai, Thailand, South Africa, Hong Kong and Italy.

Lea has just returned to the UK to have their first baby but they are planning to go off again with baby in tow in a few months' time.

They support other digital nomads with their popular locationindependent.com blog and have just launched a new blog locationindependentparents.com.

Now that the world is your office, you can live and work wherever you choose. Where would you like to go?

From worker to player

To call yourself a 'player', rather than a 'worker', is to immediately widen your conception of who you are and what you might be capable of doing. It is to dedicate yourself to realising your full human potential; to be active, not passive.

Pat Kane, ThePlayEthic.com

So what we're seeing is a new generation of people with a very different attitude to work. They are not workers but players. What exactly does that mean? Here are nine traits of players that this book will help you to understand and adopt.

1. Players put creativity, fun and fulfilment first

The worker expects work to be a chore. As players we place what really matters to us at the centre of our worlds and we fill our lives with whatever we find most exciting, enjoyable, challenging, rewarding and fulfilling. We want to indulge every aspect of ourselves. We want to play all day and get paid for it. The player's ultimate career goal is 'to get paid for being me'.

2. Players are multifaceted

> Workers take a restricted version of themselves to the office, putting on a mask for the corporate environment. Players bring all of themselves. Players are not one-dimensional beings (no human being is). Players are musicians who are also internet entrepreneurs, travellers who are also bloggers, consultants who are also songwriters, comedians who are also psychotherapists, finance administrators who are also filmmakers. We are all 'Jugglers', as author Ian Sanders calls us, managing multiple strands and projects.

3. Players respond to the world around them

> The worker thinks that play is frittering away time. But playing isn't about sitting in a corner all day daydreaming, nor is it sitting on a beach drinking cocktails for the rest of your life (that's the dream of a worker not a player). Look at what children do when they play – they are interacting with the physical world around them, testing it and experimenting with it, and they are also interacting with others and learning about relationships. Play is exploratory and responsive. To be *in play* is to be actively engaged in the world.

> A player therefore is not ignoring the real world – far from it. We are being more responsive than the worker who simply does what they're told or the business owner who follows whatever money-making strategy the latest expert recommends. Players make their lives a laboratory and learn from their own experience.

4. Players respond to their inner world

> The worker is directed by external expectations and values. As players, we recognise what is happening inside of us, accept it, acknowledge it and use it – long before others are even aware of it. The musician, music producer and artist Brian Eno said recently that the question that has occupied much of his life is 'What is it I really like?' By accepting what he discovers years before it is

fashionable to do so, he has become a thought leader who created an entire genre of music (now known as ambient). He has gone on to work with some of the biggest bands in the world including U2 and Coldplay.

5. Players are mavericks

Workers stick to the conventions of their industry or specialism. As players we indulge all our interests no matter how whimsical or disparate they may seem – sometimes resulting in misunder-standing and ridicule from others. And later we emerge with genre-smashing creative works and rule-breaking businesses. Players change the game for everyone else.

> *The truly great advances of this generation will be made by those who can make outrageous connections, and only a mind which knows how to play can do that.*
>
> **Nagle Jackson, theatre director and award-winning playwright**

Players don't know when to stop. We get obsessive about things that others barely notice. We follow paths that lead us through seemingly unrelated topics and sometimes end up in some contro-versial area of art, politics or religion. In our free exploration we tread on others' taboos. We are broader than most, more whole. We are political beings, emotional beings, sexual beings and we know how to employ all of what we are to the greatest effect.

6. Players never stop exploring, never stop learning

When children play, there is often no predetermined outcome in mind: they are simply going where they are drawn in the mo-ment. The play maps the growing edge of their human organism. Tomorrow's play will never be exactly the same as today. And then we reach adulthood and most people just stop. The worker will attend the standard company training programmes and learn some new skills for their job but they never re-enter that process of following their growing edge wherever it leads them. Players, however, remain ever curious and are hungry to learn new things. We are still willing to experiment and follow the drive in us to expand. We're engaged in a lifelong process of learning and exploring. Many of us are 'Scanners', as careers expert Barbara Sher would call us, always moving on to the next new thing. We go where we feel instinctively drawn rather than following conventional rules of success and wealth. And that path leads to true originality. In a time of information overload, we add to the signal, not to the noise.

7. Players are not naive

Players are not new-age dreamers. We play with capitalism, we notice what our market needs and we see providing value and making money as part of the game. Players understand that money makes play sustainable. And players often make *more* money than workers because we love what we do (and that passion is attractive); we are thought leaders creating original solutions; we focus on creating genuine value (not just making a quick buck); and we solve real-world problems.

8. Players surf the big waves that others are drowned by

We need to be responsive, flexible and playful right now because we are on the cusp of massive change. We're still living through the aftershocks of the near collapse of the banking system. At the same time, there is a tidal wave coming from the East as countries like China and India explode in growth. Some say we are witnessing the end of the era of economic dominance by North America and Western Europe.

As the next wave of outsourcing sweeps away any work that is easily defined and repeated, creativity will be the safest pursuit as it is specific to the local culture and environment. Now, more than ever, everything is in play and only the playful will survive.

9. Players understand that play is not effortless

Surely there's always work required to create a successful life? Well, I have a problem with the word 'work'. There are multiple meanings for the word. One meaning refers to paid employment and it's associated with that old two-state way of living between doing the things you get paid for and doing what you really enjoy in the stolen moments outside office hours. This is why we need some new vocabulary.

Another meaning of work, however, is simply the 'exertion of effort' which is still very much relevant. Play after all is not effortless: just watch a rugby match, U2 playing live, or a child building a sandcastle. Even playing a video game requires attention, concentration and persistence.

Players are engaged in something larger than the word 'work' can represent. They're creating businesses around their passion, pursuing creative and artistic experiments, starting their own social movements; they're exploring the world, what they enjoy, and what they can do. They are seeking the fullest expression of themselves. They're so passionate about what they're doing, they can't stop talking about it. What's work and what's leisure blur into one. It's all a form of play.

Take a tip from the hunter-gatherers

For all of modern society's sophistication, we could still learn something from the hunter-gatherer tribes remaining in remote locations around the world. Peter Gray is a research professor of psychology at Boston College who has studied the research on hunter-gatherer cultures. He has concluded that they do not have our concept of work as a compulsory chore. He writes on psychologytoday.com that hunter-gatherers' work is simply an extension of children's play:

> Children play at hunting, gathering, hut construction, tool making, meal preparations, defense against predators, birthing, infant care, healing, negotiation, and so on and so on; and gradually,

as their play becomes increasingly skilled, the activities become productive. The play becomes work, but it does not cease being play. It may even become more fun than before, because the productive quality helps the whole band and is valued by all.

And work is always a choice:

They deliberately avoid telling each other how to behave, in work as in any other context. [Despite this] long-term shirking apparently happens rarely if at all. It is exciting to go out hunting or gathering with the others, and it would be boring to stay in camp day after day. The fact that on any given day the work is optional and self-directed keeps it in the realm of play.

And guess what, they do fewer hours than us too:

Research studies suggest that hunter-gatherers work somewhere between 20 and 40 hours a week, on average, depending on just what you count as work. Moreover, they do not work according to the clock; they work when the time is ripe for the work to be done and when they feel like it.

It's amazing when you think about it. During the 10,000 years since the onset of agriculture and then industry, we have developed countless laborsaving devices, but we haven't reduced our labor. Today, most people spend more time working than did hunter-gatherers, and our work, on average, is less playful.

Scrap your career plan

We must be willing to get rid of the life we've planned, so as to have the life that is waiting for us.

Joseph Campbell, mythologist, writer and lecturer

The world is changing very quickly. A five-year plan for your career or business is likely to be redundant within less than a year. The CEO of Google, Eric Schmidt, recently admitted that although they have a clear mission, 'we don't have a five year plan, we don't have a 2 year plan, we don't have a 1 year plan'. And despite this Google made over $5.5 billion in just the first three months of 2009. The same rule applies even if you're just starting out; the business you start is rarely the business you end up succeeding with.

The old habit of setting far-off goals and making gross compromises in the present to get there makes less and less sense. Throw your attention back on the present and embrace 'life in perpetual beta', as new filmmaker Melissa Pierce calls it. Her documentary is exploring the cultural shift that technology creates as it enables people to live less planned and more passionate lives. And she is living her message by learning the required skills in the process of making the film and sharing content on her blog along the way.

Your long-term goals are not what will make you happy. Even getting rich is no guarantee. Research shows that when people win the lottery, they have a short-lived boost in happiness and then settle back to roughly the level of happiness they had before. What matters is how you choose to live today. Your aim in beginning to play is to create the positive experience you want to have in your life, starting right now even if it's scaled down to start with.

And ironically, pursuing your genuine interests, if done right, will make you richer than chasing the money ever will. You can't really excel at something when your heart isn't in it so if you do want to get rich, choose something that feels more like play than work. It makes good business sense; you can't compete with someone who loves what they do.

My story: 'I never want another job for the rest of my life'

Many years ago when I had a job as a computer programmer, I knew I wanted something different but didn't know what it was. I realised the only way I was really going to work it out was to imagine for a moment that I could have anything I wanted.

And what I wanted was not to work.

I didn't want to sit on the sofa all day doing nothing, I wanted to play – to do whatever creative, fun stuff I love doing, and still get paid. At the time this seemed an unrealistic desire but it wasn't long after this realisation that I got exactly what I wanted. The company announced a chance for voluntary redundancies and I jumped at it. I got paid several months of salary to go and do whatever I liked. Some of my redundant colleagues bought sports cars. I didn't. I played. I created music, did some writing and I created an installation in an experimental museum. This time of play led me into the most exciting and fun job in my career. But it was still a job.

When later I had a go at stand-up comedy, I put this into my routine:

I worry I'm in the wrong job, in fact I worry I don't suit jobs. The money's OK, it's the working I have a problem with.

I think my life is just too full to fit a job in. I'm too busy doing stuff that's actually fun and that work thing just gets in the way.

My career goal is to be paid for just being me, living my life; I'm very busy, I'm putting in the hours, I should get compensated.

Name of role . . . being John Williams.

I'd wake up in the morning and my boss would come in and go 'well done John, another great week, here's your wage packet'.

In reality this is exactly what I want; to be able to do whatever I want to do; to play all day and get paid: to get paid to be me.

Not all jobs are terrible, of course: I've had some good ones – special effects software developer, internet media specialist, senior managing consultant for a global consultancy – but whatever the job, I still felt like life was passing me by while I was stuck in front of a computer in some bland open-plan office.

In 2003 I finally escaped and publicly declared, 'I never want another job for the rest of my life'. Now I have a portfolio career consisting of careers and business mentoring, corporate creativity workshops, copywriting, blogging, internet marketing and running a monthly London event for creative people called Scanners Night. I set my own hours, choose my own co-workers and alternate my place of work between my home, my garden, the local café and a shared workspace for entrepreneurs.

Along the way I've conducted some interesting experiments: I turned a full-time job offer into a three-day-week contract paying the same money; I earned enough as a consultant to only need to work for three months of the year; I've travelled to America, Japan, South Africa and many parts of Europe on business (and often broke the old rule that you never get to see the place you work in), and I've enjoyed creative projects such as getting my experimental music played on radio stations around the world and appearing on TV news.

I still don't know what I want to do when I grow up. But I've found that the more I focus on what I enjoy doing even when it's not immediately obvious how I'll make money, the more successful I am. I'm not a millionaire but I've learned a lot about what works in my own career and those of my clients – and I know what holds people back. My mission to get paid to play continues to evolve; it's not a project that is ever done. But it's one that I hope to convince you to start.

Let's talk about death

It might seem strange to bring death into a book about play but in fact it is at the very heart of the topic. Here's a defining event from my life that I think will show you why.

When I was 5 months old, my parents took me out with my brother in the family car to show me to some relatives. Just a few minutes from our home, we were hit head-on by a young drunk driver who had lost control and was on the wrong side of the road.

Both my parents were injured. My mother made a full recovery. My father died in hospital ten days later from complications with his injuries. He was 34.

Losing my father before I was even old enough to know him has coloured my whole life. It made it abundantly and painfully clear that life can end at any moment. With this stark reality in mind, now answer this question: do you really want to spend another few years doing some unsatisfying work in the hope that you can do what you really like later?

Here's the real message of this book:

DON'T WASTE ANOTHER MINUTE OF YOUR LIFE

What do you really want your life to be about? This book will show you how to start it right now. If you don't know what you want, your mission is to find out. This book will tell you how. It's less important that you complete your work mission than that you're engaged in it. It's in the *being in play* that you will find salvation. When you are fully engaged in the right project, you will easily attract others around you who are inspired by the same aims. And if the worst happens and you don't get to complete your work yourself, others will pick up the reins.

Do what really matters. Start playing. Start now.

Apple CEO Steve Jobs came to a similar conclusion:

When I was 17, I read a quote that went something like 'If you live each day as if it was your last, someday you'll most certainly be right.' It made an impression on me, and since then, for the past 33 years, I have looked in the mirror every morning and asked myself, 'If today were the last day of my life, would I want to do what I am about to do today?' And whenever the answer has been no for too many days in a row, I know I need to change something.

Remembering that I'll be dead soon is the most important tool I've ever encountered to help me make the big choices in life. Because almost everything – all external expectations, all pride, all fear of embarrassment or failure – these things just fall away in the face of death, leaving only what is truly important. Remembering that you are going to die is the best way I know to avoid the trap of thinking you have something to lose. You are already naked. There is no reason not to follow your heart.

Steve Jobs, CEO of Apple Inc. and former CEO of Pixar Animation Studios

The first step in your journey to getting paid to play is to find out what you really want. The next chapter will show you how to discover what that is.

On the website ScrewWorkLetsPlay.com

➡ Read and listen to interviews with ten successful players.

➡ Access more information and website links for the people quoted in this chapter.

➡ Connect with a global community of players.

Secret one

How to work out what you really really want

Too much of a good thing can be wonderful.

Mae West, American actress, playwright and screenwriter 1893–1980

The very first step to getting paid to play is to know what feels like play to you. You'll find out what that is in this chapter. And I'll show you that, no matter how impossible your ideas might seem right now, you can always have what you really really want.

If you already enjoy your work and just want to become more successful at it, you may be tempted to skip this chapter. Don't! If your work has never quite taken off, there's a good chance it's because what you're doing is not quite right yet. This chapter will help you correct your course so that you focus in on what's most enjoyable and easy for you and so get much better results for the same effort.

For the love of chocolate

Petra Barran's Choc Star is Britain's only touring choc-mobile: a converted ice cream van serving gourmet chocolate treats. Choc Star travels from market to music festival to private party much to the delight of its customers. But how did Petra come up with the idea?

My main things in life have always been love of travel and love of new people and love of food. And I've been searching my whole life for a way of turning this into something that gets me up in the morning and makes me a living; well actually, makes me a life as much as a living.

I've tried lots of different things. When I finished university I thought, 'I'm going to become a casting director.' And I worked for some casting directors in London, looking for people for parts in TV commercials and pop videos and I used to have to go up to strangers in the street and say 'Hey, you'd be great for this part.' I loved it but I still had itchy feet. I just wanted to get out there and explore the world. So I decided to run away to sea. I worked on super yachts all over the world looking after very rich people; making them cocktails and making their beds and serving them dinner. And that was fantastic but life onboard was just a little too strict and controlled for me.

While I was away I noticed that wherever I went, I was always drawn to chocolate shops. Whether I was in America or Spain or France or Israel I was always hanging out in chocolate shops looking at what everyone else was doing. And eventually I decided, right, enough is enough. I've got to stop working on boats. I decided to go back to London with this idea that I wanted to work with chocolate and it needed to be something that allowed me to keep on moving and meeting new people. I was going to set up a chocolate business. I just decided, right, I'm going to get a van and I'm going to turn it into a choc-mobile and I'm going to take it around the world.

Read more of the Choc Star story at *chocstar.co.uk*

Start from the right place

When we're trying to decide what we really want, the old-fashioned idea of work as something we have to do, rather than want to do, can all too easily get in the way. We make unnecessary compromises and limit our choices right from the start. If we become desperate to escape our current work we can end up looking for anything that seems an improvement. But that's like asking, 'What's not quite as bad as this?' This is starting from the wrong place if you want to end up playing for a living. And it's a lousy question to invest your energy answering.

Here's a much better question to ask yourself: 'What would work that feels like play look like for me?'

To answer it, you have to imagine you could have anything in the world. Seriously; anything. Put aside all practicalities, just for a while, and allow yourself to dream. If you've got stuck trying to work out what to do next, I can guarantee it's because you have failed to separate the questions 'What do I want?' and 'What seems possible for me right now?' Concentrate for now on the first one and we'll work out how to make it happen, or at least get as close as possible, a little later. It's essential to your success that you allow yourself to want things that you currently have no idea how you will get.

> *If you limit your choices only to what seems possible or reasonable, you disconnect yourself from what you truly want, and all that is left is a compromise.*
>
> **Robert Fritz, composer, filmmaker and organisational consultant**

One of the most valuable things you can ever do is to get to know what you do and don't enjoy doing. And it can also be one of the most difficult things to do. Believe it or not, actually getting to where you want to go can seem relatively straightforward after that! It's just a list of stuff to do – call someone, write an email, turn up somewhere and do the work. If you hit an obstacle, someone will be able to tell you how to get around it.

When you know what comes most naturally to you and then centre your working life around it, leaving out as much as possible of what you don't like, you will be amazed how fast your progress can be. Your work will be like play, your passion will attract new opportunities to you every day, and your competitors will barely concern you.

Introducing your secret weapon: your playbook

Don't wait to be hit by a lightning bolt insight on what you're meant to be doing with your life. Understand instead that decisions like this are more usually built than happened upon. Build your path to playing brick by brick.

Get yourself a notebook to capture your thoughts about your transition from worker to player. Carry it everywhere. Write down everything you discover – what you like, what you don't like, people whose work or lifestyle you'd like to emulate, ideas for contacts to talk to, projects to try. This is now your *playbook*. Choose a nicely designed blank book for the purpose: one that will inspire you every time you look at it. Free yourself from the tyranny of lined paper and buy an unlined book. It allows more freedom to draw diagrams, doodles and sketches (you're not in school and no one is going to criticise your handwriting if it isn't straight). Label your playbook and add your phone number in case it gets lost; this is an important document.

Keep these notes separate from your other thoughts – don't mix them with your diary, your creative writing or your laundry list. You need to be able to leaf through it quickly and find something that you wrote earlier.

This brings us to the first of our 21 myths that keep you stuck.

Myth 1: If it's important, you'll remember it

Don't believe it! Even if it was true, why would you want to fill your brain up with stuff to remember when you should be leaving it clear for thinking? By recording your ideas as they occur, and not straining to find 'the answer' straight away, you'll find that important insights will unfold naturally within your notes.

Richard Branson organises his 200-plus businesses using simple black ledger notebooks; 'I can't believe when I see people not writing things down. You know they're not going to remember everything', he says. His advice is to 'Always carry a little notebook in your back pocket . . . Make sure you use it for ideas, for contacts, for suggestions, for problems . . . Your life will be that much better organized for carrying it. I could never have built the Virgin Group into the size it is without those few bits of paper.' He now has over a hundred black ledger notebooks that he's written in over the years.

'Just one more thing . . .', or what Columbo can teach you about discovering what you really want

I love the detective show *Columbo*. It's the ultimate wind-down TV: slow-paced and charming. The series has been running for over 30 years but the classics are from the 1970s, featuring mutton chop sideburns and plots that revolve around 'cutting-edge technology' like telephone answering machines.

Lieutenant Columbo, played by Peter Falk, is a homicide detective with the Los Angeles Police Department. Every feature length episode starts with showing the actual murder scene. There is therefore no mystery, no whodunit. The pleasure is in watching Columbo, the disheveled, apologetic cop, shambling his way towards snaring his prey and proving them guilty.

Columbo knows in the first scene who the murderer is but doesn't let on to his subject. His talent is in appearing to be harmless, enabling him to bypass the murderer's defences, while he gathers fragments of evidence that point to what really happened. Nothing goes unmissed no matter how small: a single word, a piece of lint, a sound on a recording. He jots it all down in his notebook. Columbo is troubled by details he can't resolve and he drives his suspect to distraction with his famous line 'Just one more thing . . .'.

When you are on a search to discover what you'd like to do with your life, you can learn a lot from Columbo. It's time to play detective in 'The case of the missing passion'. Your adversary is your inner critic or 'top dog' (see Secret four).

Put yourself under surveillance. No clue should go unnoticed. What part of the newspaper do you turn to first? What part of a bookshop draws you? What are your favourite TV programmes? What do you read for fun? What did you enjoy doing as a child? What kind of environment inspires you? What kind of people do you naturally get on with? What kind of daily structure suits you? What's your MO – your habits and style of working? This is all information you can use to help you on your path to play.

The evidence is there. Follow every lead; act on your hunches. This is what Petra did in her story at the start of this chapter; she acted on her hunches, played them out, and then noticed what her responses were. She knew she loved travel, food, and meeting new people. When she noticed herself being drawn to chocolate shops, the last piece of the puzzle fell into place.

Carry your playbook everywhere and record every piece of evidence about what work you do like and what work you don't. Look for where the excitement is in you. Just remember that it often comes with a big dollop of fear too! We'll look at this later. If you hit a dead end, call for back-up – get help from friends or have a session with a careers or business coach.

(By the way, I think this finally shows that it's possible to turn anything that you enjoy, including lying on the sofa watching reruns on TV, into something useful for your business!)

> ### Myth 2: The answer to my work search is in some magical new thing I have never tried before
>
> If you're currently trapped in a job, you may be prone to thinking that there is some kind of work out there you have never tried before that is the magic solution to your dilemma. The fact is if you really love doing something, you're probably already doing it somewhere in your life; you just might not see it as something you consider work. Start the process of noting everything you enjoy and later you will see how you can get paid for it.

Stop trying to work out what to do with the rest of your life

Here's the good news: you don't need to know what you want to do with the rest of your life. In fact, asking yourself questions like that is more likely to keep you stuck. There's no way to know what you'll want in ten years' time because you won't be the same person you are now. What you do in your very next step will take you in directions you could never have predicted and reveal new aspects of yourself you're not even aware of right now.

Let's think a little more short term. Here's an exercise that will help you get a lot closer to discovering what you really want to do.

Let's take a year out

How would you like to take a year off? Let's say the whole of the next 12 months. Sounds appealing? OK, I hereby give you my permission. Done.

Yes, I know you have a few practical concerns like what you'll live on but let's dream a little. Imagine I'd just handed you a year's salary so you don't need to earn anything. Think about this for a moment – next Friday is now your last day in your current work. Now, what is it you're going to do in this precious year of total freedom? Spend a year sitting on the beach, doing nothing? Or do you know that after the first few weeks, you'd be itching to do something else? If so, what? What exactly *will* you do for the other 11 months?

Maybe you'll do some projects you've been wanting to do for a long time: write a book; record an album; start your own business; write a blog; go study something you're fascinated by; travel the world; do up your home; get serious about your photography; have your own exhibition; become a public speaker; get into TV; go work alongside a hero of yours; or change some piece of the world for the better.

Or perhaps now you're free of work, you'll take the time to address some part of your personal life: cure that rumbling medical gripe, work out how to make yourself genuinely happy, create a fulfilling relationship, or heal a rift in your family?

Whatever it might be, at 5 p.m. next Friday you are free at last. What will you do?

Among my clients, Philip would 'build a kick-arse inventor workshop'; Sally would 'fiddle with things, make things, and spend time inspiring people'; Neil would be studying Integral Philosophy; Juliette would sail across the Atlantic and blog about it; and Emma would be living by the sea, with a pet dog and indulging her love of flower photography.

Write it down. Turn to a blank page in your playbook (or grab the nearest scrap of paper – don't get precious about this) and write down all the things you would like to do in your year of play. If anything requires more money than is available in your annual salary, I am granting you a limitless fund for any experience you want to have. This is not about buying new shiny things, it's so that there is nothing in the way of having the experiences you want – round-the-world air ticket, money to buy that castle you want to renovate; it's all possible now.

Of course, when you begin your year of total freedom you might just want to take a long holiday or catch up with friends. Make a note of this, but then start to think of what you might do after a couple of months of chill-out and catch-up.

Need a little more inspiration?

Still sketchy about what projects you'd take on in your year of play? Here are five questions to consider that will help spark your creative engine.

Looking back over your career, when were you most happy?

Write down any moments that occur to you. It may have been something that was not a central part of your work but you really enjoyed anyway: organising the Christmas party, competing in the office football league. Write it down, then think about what it was that made this so enjoyable for you. You might choose to include some element of this in your year out.

Who is your career hero?

Is there someone whose life or work you really admire? Who is it? It could be someone famous, someone from history, someone you know or even someone fictional. What is it about them you most admire? Is it the field they work in, the results they create or the attitude they have that you're impressed by? What project or achievement of theirs stands out for you? Write it all down in your playbook. If several people come to mind, write them all down.

One of my career heroes is musician, producer, visual artist and creative thinker Brian Eno. He once wrote a diary for a year and published it as a book. He wrote in the introduction, 'I have a wonderful life. I do pretty much what I want, and the only real problem I ever have is wondering what that is.' His career is enormously varied. He is very successful and hugely respected in his field, yet almost unheard of by the majority of the population and so is free to walk down the street unnoticed. This sounds like the ideal working life to me. What's yours? What elements of their lives would you want to re-create in your year of freedom?

Who do you envy?

Whose working life are you envious of? What aspect of this person's work makes you most envious? When I am helping clients with their careers or businesses I very occasionally get envious of them. The two times that stand out for me were with people moving into working for large cutting-edge creative agencies. These are high-profile organisations that are tough to get into. One client resorted to baking a cake for the company and writing his CV in icing on the top just to get an interview. (It worked.)

Envy is a useful thing. It tells me there's something I still don't have. In this case, I worked out that I needed to bring more of my love of design into my work. I've done this by working with great designers to help create the brand of several businesses, and compiling a simple blog of contemporary design images just for fun.

Sometimes envy will reveal something you can't access any other way. Ask people what's their ideal work and a lot of people are stumped. Ask whose job/business/lifestyle they most envy and you get some useful information. As long as you don't stay with the envy and imagine you're powerless to have the thing you want, you can use it.

Envy implies that you want something that is out of reach to you. Recognising the envy is useful if you can remove the block to getting it. To do this, imagine hiring the very person you envy to train you step by step to get the thing you want. What advice do you think they would give you? What would they need to teach you? Perhaps you'd need to borrow some of their resources and contacts too. With all this at your disposal, what project would you now take on? Write it down.

What do you find difficult to stop doing?

What do you hate not to be doing? What do you find yourself squeezing into stolen moments? What is difficult for you to stop doing when you should be getting on with your work? Write it all down. Which of these would you do more of in your year out? (Now imagine you could get paid for doing this – Lindsey Mountford did exactly this when she found a way to get paid for playing around on Facebook and watching YouTube videos – read her story in the next chapter.)

What project(s) would you take on if you knew you couldn't fail?

Write a novel? Become a rock star? Climb the Matterhorn? Find a cure for cancer? Overthrow the government? Write down your answer. Add some version of it into your year off. No matter how grand your dream, there will be a way to have a taste of it.

Too many things to do to fit into one year?

By this point, you may be looking at your notes and feeling alarmed at the number of things you want to do!

Myth 3: I should be able to find one thing that interests me and stick to it

The traditional world of work tries to cram everything that we are into a narrow box and give it a single label: programmer, accountant, designer, writer. We are all far more than one label can contain: we are 'slashes': programmer/social activist; accountant/business coach; interior designer/TV personality/musician; writer/public speaker/parent . . . and more.

▶

> When you design a working life from scratch, there is no need to hide away any part of you any more. As a player, you can bring all of who you are to your work and be all the more valuable as a result.

Your interests will naturally change, evolve and expand over time. As they do, you can reposition your work to suit. It's possible that what you're currently doing was once exciting and challenging but now feels dull. That's natural. The most exciting projects and tasks are always at the edge of our abilities; once we've mastered them, they lose their shine and we're ready for the next thing.

We each have a different pace at which we like to evolve our work. What's yours? Are you happy to go deep into a topic and specialise for several years before you move on? Or do you get bored easily and have to keep switching to something new to keep your interest? If you're in the latter group who likes to chop and change frequently, you're what US careers guru Barbara Sher calls a 'Scanner'.

Are you a Scanner?

➡ Are you interested in lots of different, and seemingly unrelated things?

➡ Are you fascinated by something different every week?

➡ Does the thought of concentrating on one topic, skill or job for very long horrify you?

➡ Do you start lots of projects but move on before you finish them?

If you answered yes to more than one of these then you are almost certainly a Scanner. A Scanner is someone who loves to learn and explore new things but gets bored quickly. Scanners are about breadth rather than depth. We want to learn just enough about something to understand the most interesting bits of it and then move on to the next thing.

Scanners are also sometimes referred to as Renaissance men/women, just like the most famous Scanner of all, Leonardo da Vinci. Leonardo was a scientist, mathematician, engineer, inventor, anatomist, painter, sculptor, architect, botanist, musician and writer. And he often didn't finish the projects he started; so if that sounds like you, you're in good company.

Entrepreneurs are often Scanners, using their enthusiasm for starting things to good effect.

'I get really into things and then I get bored'

Sophie Boss runs her business Beyond Chocolate with her sister Audrey, helping women to stop dieting and overeating and finally enjoy food without guilt, and lose weight. Sophie started the business after many years of failing to find a job that would keep her interest:

> I was the kind of person who, even as a child, loved learning how to do new things I'd find out how to do them, would do them passionately for a while, and then I'd get bored. Knitting, sewing, photography, cooking; you name it, I'd have a go. I'd get really into it for a while and then once I'd mastered it I found it boring and I would move on to something else. I did that with my jobs as well. I left university and was recruited into management at a well-known high street retailer. I did really well, reached the top and thought 'This has got to be the most boring job I've ever done'. I went and sold advertising. Became pretty good at that too. It was the late 80s, boom time, so I made lots of money but I found it desperately tedious and looked around for something else to excite me. So I decided to retrain as a teacher. I absolutely adored doing that for a while. I loved the excitement of a new project. I was on top of the world, and then a year or two years in I'd be bored because the excitement

would wear off. I didn't know about Scanners and I didn't know
that this was okay, because actually what I told myself was 'I'm
never going to be happy doing anything'.

It was setting up her own business with her sister Audrey that finally
held her interest:

Now, by having my own business, I can do whatever I like. I take
the business in the directions that excite me. We are constantly
developing new projects and once we master them we create
new ones!

Read more about Beyond Chocolate at *beyondchocolate.co.uk*

Whether you're a Scanner or you like to dive deep into a topic for
longer, the important thing is to craft a life that suits you. If you like
to specialise, your year off might be about throwing yourself into a
year of intense study. If you're a Scanner, it will be about choosing
a project (or projects) that will retain your interest. They should
be multifaceted, have lots of new things to learn, and allow you to
use your skill to come up with new ideas or do research without
having to do all the implementation yourself. Scanners make great
journalists, comedians, consultants, public speakers, research-
ers and inventors – anything that maximises the ability to learn
quickly, make creative connections, communicate what we found,
and move on. Find other people to do the follow-through work like
detailed editing, project planning or financial management.

And if the thought of choosing only one year off is stressing you
out, read on for an exercise that will help.

Welcome to the universe(s)

I have an uncle who is an astrophysicist and works at large ob-
servatories around the world. I was on the phone to him one

Christmas and trying to think of something to talk about with this very intelligent but rather introverted man. Running out of small talk, I asked, 'So what's new in physics?' After a considerable silent pause while he gathered his thoughts, he said in his slow, doleful, voice, 'Well . . . there's a lot of interest at the moment in wormholes between parallel universes'. 'Wait a minute, back up a bit', I said, 'are you telling me there are parallel universes?' 'Well yes, that's the best thinking at the current time', he calmly replied. Somehow this rather incredible information had not ended up on the front page of the newspapers.

Some experts in quantum physics go as far as to suggest that every time a decision is made, the universe splits into two – one where the first choice plays out and another where the opposite choice plays out. We don't yet know how to move between these worlds, but until my uncle cracks it, it's a very useful idea to consider. Because now you don't just have one year off, you have infinite variations of your year off.

Let's just take the first seven of them. Realising you can live seven completely different years off, write down what you will do in each one. In universe one you might become an entrepreneur and get rich; in universe two perhaps you travel to India and pursue your spiritual development; in universe three you could become a full-time parent; in universe four you become a social activist; in universe five a full-time artist – and you still have two left. Write them all down in your playbook.

But isn't all this totally unrealistic? A little bit. But you can have what you want a lot more often than you think. If you don't at least know what you want, what chance do you have of getting it? And even if you can't have exactly what you want, you'll get a lot closer by knowing what it is.

Here's the good news: you can have what you *really* want

Here's the thing: no matter how crazy your dream is of getting paid to play, you can always have the part you really want. Even if you can't have the exact vision you see in your mind, you will be able to have the part that's most exciting to you as long as you're flexible about how you get it.

Here's the critical question most people never ask themselves: what is the *experience* you want to have in this vision of your ideal work? Plenty of people might have the same dream – for instance, to be a rock star – but the reasons will differ. What's the part you really want? What's the experience of being a rock star that matters to you? For some it's performing in front of an audience and being the centre of attention; for some it's being rich; for others it's being creative, or it's the status of being known and respected, or it's being a rebel, or touring the country with a group, or controlling your own life. (And for some I guess it's the sex and drugs but we'll leave that to one side for now.)

Once you know what the experience is that you really want, you can be sure you will get it when you go for the dream. And even more importantly, if you decide not to go for your original dream, there are then many ways you can have the part you want most.

Imagine a lawyer who dreams of being a rock star. He realises he loves the reliable salary of a job so decides not to risk it all for rock stardom. Instead, he goes and gets a job in the legal department of a record company because that seems a good alternative. The problem is that the experience of his job is largely the same; what he does day to day hasn't changed. He still sits in an office and writes contracts all day but now every so often Madonna walks past his desk. If the experience he wants is to perform in front of an audience, he might find that getting a slot on TV as a legal expert or giving talks at major conferences is far more satisfying.

Back to you. Write down in your playbook the experience you want to have when you think of your dream work. What's the essence of your ideal vision that's most important to you? What's the most exciting part? Be completely honest with yourself and don't worry what anyone else might think – if you want to be world famous, or you want to get rich, or you realise that the most exciting thing in the world to you is to pore over 30 pages of financial figures, don't let anyone else's opinion of what's selfish or superficial or weird or boring get in the way. Just write it down.

Myth 4: I can't do what I want to do without a long expensive training

A common stumbling block is that what you want to do requires a long and expensive training. If you don't want to do this or can't afford it, with some creativity you can usually think of a different way to get the experience you want to have. Get clear what the part is that you're most drawn to and find a different way to get that without the long training.

We get stuck when we think it's the dream or nothing. In fact, the dream is just a signpost to an experience you want more of. It's an indicator of what you need for the next stage of your own development. And this development is a natural part of being human that continues throughout our lives if we don't block it. You might find at one point in your life that you feel drawn to leading a team, or climbing to the top of the corporate ladder. And once you've had that experience, you might then be drawn to go and work for yourself. Each experience builds on the last and it's impossible to tell in advance where the next one will lead you. If you ignore whatever is your current itch, you won't get to find out just what interesting places it might take you.

Some of what you've written in these exercises might surprise you; it might seem kind of random right now. Just trust that if you can find a way to have the experience you want next, you will keep moving towards work that is more satisfying – and you'll keep developing as a person. All living organisms have this same drive towards growth and self-expression: a tree will keep growing to its full genetic potential as long as it has the space and the sustenance it needs.

> *Musicians must make music, artists must paint, poets must write if they are to be ultimately at peace with themselves. What human beings can be, they must be.*
>
> **Abraham Maslow, American psychologist, 1908–1970**

When you are truly in play, when you are following the unfolding path of what provides you engagement, expression, excitement and curiosity in the world, then your work is simply a natural expression of who you are and who you are becoming. This is the revolutionary shift from living as a worker to living as a player. Work becomes a way of achieving the fullest expression of yourself. At its deepest level, it's a channel, as author David Deida says, for giving your love to the world.

So if you ask, 'Can I really have what I want in my work?', the answer is of course you can, because everyone can move towards their fullest expression of themselves; everyone can decide to give their love to the world in their work. The only person blocking you from doing that is you. Open your mind and you'll see there's always a way to have the experience you are craving in your work. And you'll see later how you can guarantee you get it.

Introducing Play Wednesday

Here's an exercise that will help you envision your life of play in detail and let you have a taste of it right now.

Let's zoom in on your year of play. Fast forward three months and imagine you're well into your year of freedom. You've got the life you've always wanted and you're having a ball. It's Wednesday, and a particularly excellent Wednesday at that. What does it look like? Where are you living? What time do you get up? What do you do first? What time do you start your activities for the day? Where do you go to do them? What are you doing? Who with? What happens the rest of the day? What time do you finish? What do you do afterwards? Write it all down in your playbook.

Of course, you probably can't take the whole year off work in reality, but you can begin to build some of that ideal experience into your life right now. Wednesday is a great day to experiment with this. Halfway between weekends, it's the ideal time to build a little play into your work week.

Make Wednesday every week a day when you get a little bit closer to your ideal life. Take some time first thing in the morning, or in the afternoon if you have the option, or in the evening after work. Note it in your diary to remind yourself every week. Even if you can only grab a few minutes out of your day, do it. If you want to be a poet, take a book of poems to read and a notebook to write in on your commute. If you're excited about share dealing, make a little time to read the financial news or a book on the stock market. Then find ways to free up more time as the weeks go on so you can get closer to your ideal. Why not really throw yourself into it and take the day off to try living as you would like? If your dream is to live by the sea, take a trip to the coast and spend a day living like a local. Exercises where individuals design their ideal day and then set about creating it have been scientifically proven to add to your happiness, so it's well worth doing!

In the next chapter you'll find out how to choose what to do next to bring you a step closer to making your vision of a year out a reality.

Put it into play

Keys to this secret:

➡ Start thinking with a blank slate about what you really really want; imagine your year of play and write it down.

➡ Don't wait for inspiration; build your decision: write down everything you discover about what you do and don't want in your work.

➡ Get clear what the experience is that you really want to have. There is always a way to have this.

What you should have now:

➡ a vision of your ideal working life;

➡ some idea of the experience you want to have from the next stage of your working life.

Take ten minutes to play:

➡ Open your diary and write in a time to go and buy yourself a playbook.

➡ Write Play Wednesday in your diary as a repeating appointment to live a little of your year out.

➡ Live a little of your year of play right now; give yourself a small taste today of what your year of play would be about. You may need to apply some seriously lateral thinking to do so. If you would be living in Japan but right now it seems impossible, get yourself a novel to read that's set in the country; watch films and documentaries about the place; eat the food; listen to Japanese music; book yourself a language course, or go to a language exchange evening.

It's not meant to be a substitute for the real thing, but it will give you a taste; it will engage your creativity and, hopefully, leave you in a happy and positive state of mind – which is the best possible state in which to make real changes to your life. In the next chapter, we'll look at how to get you a little closer to the real year-off experience.

Exclusive extras on ScrewWorkLetsPlay.com

➡ more information for Scanners and details of monthly workshops;

➡ interviews with Petra Barran talking about Choc Star and Sophie Boss talking about Beyond Chocolate;

➡ access to expert coaches for some one-to-one help.

Secret two
How to choose what to do next

Where the needs of the world and your talents cross, there lies your vocation.

Aristotle 348–322BC

You should now have some ideas for what you would do with your time if you had complete freedom. You've looked at the things you enjoy doing and the experiences you want to have. But how does all this translate into a possible direction for your work? And how do you know which thread to pursue? This chapter will help you pick a direction to investigate further. Here's a great story about just such a career decision.

Paul McCartney, coil winder

In 1961 Paul McCartney had a choice to make: to keep his safe job as a coil winder in a Liverpool factory or to pursue his dreams with The Beatles. He explains what happened next:

I started working at a coil-winding factory called Massey and Coggins. My dad had told me to go out and get a job. I'd said, 'I've got a job, I'm in a band.' But after a couple of weeks of doing nothing with the band it was, 'No, you have got to get a proper job.' He virtually chucked me out of the house. So I went to the employment office and said, 'Can I have a job? Just give me anything.' And the first job was sweeping the yard at Massey and Coggins. I took it.

I went there and the personnel officer said, 'We can't have you sweeping the yard, you're management material.' And they started to train me from the shop floor up with that in mind. Of course, I wasn't very good on the shop floor – I wasn't a very good coil-winder.

One day John and George showed up in the yard that I should have been sweeping and told me we had a gig at the Cavern. I said, 'No. I've got a steady job here and it pays £7 14s a week. They are training me here. That's pretty good, I can't expect more.' And I was quite serious about this.

But then . . . I thought, 'Sod it. I can't stick this lot.' I bunked over the wall and was never seen again by Massey and Coggins. Pretty shrewd move really, as things turned out.

Paul McCartney from *The Beatles Anthology*

It takes bravery to dare to do what you really want to do. And you may need to challenge some of the popular myths about work, like the following old classic.

Myth 5: Doing what you love is selfish

One of the most destructive myths in life is that doing what you love to do and steering away from the things you don't is being selfish. But remember that we enjoy doing the things that we are good at. And we are drawn to the things that are most important to the next stage of our development as human beings.

When you hold back from using your unique mix of talents, you actually short-change your company, your clients and even the human race. That is being selfish. And everybody loses; you impoverish the world. What would have happened if Paul McCartney had stayed working as a rather unmotivated coil-winder and written off his part in The Beatles as self-indulgent nonsense? Who knows if you'll reach the dizzying heights that Paul did? It doesn't matter. Better for everyone that you do what you're really good at and love to do than be yet another example of mediocrity.

Remember it's not all about you. If you're a blocked artist, or you've written something but never shown it to anyone, or you've got an idea to improve your industry but you think you're not qualified to make suggestions, it's easy to get wound up in your own internal battle. But it's not just about you. Everyone misses out when you hold back. Maybe your first bit of writing won't be fantastic, but it will lay the foundations for your next piece. And if nothing else, when you dare to do something you care about, you inspire others to do what they care about.

Staying in ill-fitting work is detrimental to your happiness. Your self-esteem is dependent on feeling capable and if all the feedback about your work is negative, you won't feel that. It's important to start making your shift into something better suited as soon as you can.

How do you know what to invest your time in playing? Well firstly, playing at whatever you feel drawn to regardless of potential income – pure play – is a valuable pursuit in itself, at least for a while. Why? Because it's fun (and fun is good for you); it gets you into motion; it helps you discover what you like (and what you don't); what you're good at (and what you're not so good at); and it develops new skills and emerging aspects of your personality that can grow into a whole new direction for your life. If you've been stuck for a long time on what to do next in your work, and you can afford some time for experimentation, it's worth choosing almost anything you're really keen to do and having a play with it for a few weeks.

But how do you ensure you can eventually get paid and you don't just play your way to poverty? The key is that some of your play must meet a need that people have. Besides, the latest psychological research shows that the happiest people in the world use their natural strengths in the service of others.

The happiness equation

Want to know the magic formula for a happy and fulfilling life? Here it is:

Pleasure + Engagement + Meaning = Happiness.

Pleasure is experiencing positive emotions from enjoying activities and relationships: a great meal, riding your bike, a picnic in the park with someone you love. And it's also the ability to notice and savour these experiences as they happen. Just recalling a positive experience that happened to you yesterday has been shown to make you measurably happier.

Engagement is the experience of getting lost in something you find so satisfying that you lose track of time and hours fly by in moments. It's being in play, absorbed in those activities you imagined in your year out.

Meaning is about using your strengths in the service of a cause greater than yourself; making a contribution to something beyond the boundaries of your own life.

To be both happy and satisfied with your life, you need all three of these elements. We often mistakenly believe pleasure is all you need to be happy but in fact the good feelings from pleasurable experiences tend not to last very long. When the experience is over, the good feelings quickly subside. However, being in service, doing something good for others brings good feelings that persist after the event is over.

When you're immersed in something that feels like play, you are likely to experience both pleasure and engagement. The third element is to use your play to help others. If you want to get paid to play, connecting with the needs of others will ensure you don't play your way to poverty.

Here's the thing. As soon as we start talking about helping others, a whole lot of 'shoulds' appear and we start imagining that we must volunteer to make tea at the old folks' home or go live in a mud hut in deepest Africa. We fall into the do-gooder trap. If you like doing those things, go do them; otherwise find another way to support the same cause. This is supposed to be fun, remember? What I'm talking about here is doing what you genuinely enjoy *and* finding a way to help others while doing it. Read on for a simple exercise that will help you find a way to do this. It might just change the entire focus of your work.

Find your moment

There are already moments in your life when you use your natural strengths to help others. Think back to a recent time in your work that stands out as a great moment: one when you did something you know you are great at, you really enjoyed doing it, and it had a positive impact. What were you doing at that moment? What made it so enjoyable for you?

Your moment may come in many different forms – coming up with the new idea that makes a whole project run better; making a great joke in the middle of a presentation; saying something encouraging to a co-worker when they most need it; negotiating a huge discount on a purchase; pointing someone to just the right piece of information; tweaking a process or system to make it better; finding a clever way to automate a task; spotting the error in a plan before it starts. Look for something you got a great deal of pleasure out of – not just for the result (like a pat on the back from your boss or client) – but in the actual doing of it.

This moment may not be something that is in your job description or main business tasks – setting up your PC for maximum productivity or writing a funny email for a colleague's birthday. If your current work is so off the mark that you can't think of a single moment of this kind, look at your personal life for moments when you do something brilliantly, enjoy it and it's valuable to other people. Often this thing took you very little time at all to do – even if a huge amount of experience and preparation led up to it.

This is your *moment of magic.* Write it down in your playbook. Think of two or three other moments that stand out and write these down too. Can you see any common element that makes them so special to you? Write it down if so, but don't worry if not.

Now here's a thought. How often are you doing your moment of magic currently in your work? Once a day? Once a week? Once a month? Only in your spare time? Imagine if you just did your moment of magic twice as often in a week. How much more valuable would you be to your employer or your business? You might find you were twice as valuable. Now imagine expanding this moment so that your whole career revolves around it and your working week centres on having these moments. How much fun would that be? How valuable would you be? Can you see that it might be possible for you to get paid for all that value?

How to get into flow – an introduction to Wealth Dynamics

Your moment of magic is you at your best; it's an experience of being in flow. This means doing those things that you are naturally talented at and enjoy doing. To get paid to play, you must spend as much time as possible in flow. Personality profiling is excellent to help you do this. If we all knew ourselves thoroughly and were totally in touch with what we liked and didn't like, we wouldn't need personality-profiling systems: we would know exactly what work we should each be doing. Meanwhile, in the real world, we can benefit from something that shows us our best traits and the patterns of the work that does and doesn't suit us.

My favourite personality-profiling system (particularly for anyone who is or who wants to be self-employed) is Wealth Dynamics.

Wealth Dynamics is a powerful personality-profiling system and philosophy of entrepreneurship created by serial entrepreneur, Roger Hamilton. Roger owns and runs successful businesses in publishing, property, event management, training and franchising.

Wealth Dynamics does not tell you what job you should do or what business you should run. Instead it shows you the part you should play in any business or project. This is your 'path of least resistance'. When you stick to it, work feels like play and you achieve success, wealth and impact quicker and with far less effort.

Want to know which Wealth Profile is yours? There are eight profiles, each with its own path of least resistance. Read the descriptions below and see which one sounds like you. To know for sure, you can take an online test.

Creator

Strengths: big-picture thinking; starting projects and businesses; creating products; coming up with new ideas; brainstorming; inventing; innovating. Creators get wealthy from creating products and businesses that others manage and deliver.

Weaknesses: focusing on one project and following through to finish it; managing finances, teams; doing admin.

Star

Strengths: standing out from the crowd; being in the limelight; presenting, performing. Also good at drawing out the best in products, businesses or environments – interior designer, graphic designer, marketing or branding expert. Often good at bringing out the best in people – as coach, motivational speaker or personal stylist. Stars create wealth by creating a brand.

Weaknesses: may value image over execution; quick to spend.

Supporter

Strengths: interpersonal skills and building relationships; talking to new people, motivating teams, helping others excel without needing to be in the limelight themselves; taking the wild ideas of a creator and turning them into projects and action plans. Supporters create wealth by supporting an entrepreneurial Creator or by leading a team to excel.

Weaknesses: financial spreadsheets, technical details, being chained to a desk. Prefer face-to-face interactions to email and online.

Deal maker

Strengths: communication, influence and negotiaton; spotting connections in the market; wheeling and dealing; wining and dining; strong sense of timing. Likes to be on the phone and on the move. Practical and down to earth. Create their wealth in deals between other people.

Weaknesses: sticking to a plan; innovating new ideas.

Trader

Strengths: buying low and selling high, whether getting a bargain at the flea market or trading shares on the stock market. Extrovert traders are good at hard bargaining. Introvert traders prefer to trade through analysis. Traders have been trading all their life – haggling for a discount or experimenting with a market stall. May love travel and languages and be drawn to importing and exporting goods. Great sense of timing, observant, grounded, and can multitask.

Weaknesses: may spread themselves too thinly.

Accumulator

Strengths: detail-oriented; following systems and procedures; being reliable, meticulous and delivering on time; playing it safe; spotting what might go wrong in a project. Create wealth by playing the long game; accumulating shares, property, assets. Or helping keep a team grounded, ensuring that everything is in order and that what needs to get done gets done on time.

Weaknesses: may procrastinate; gets distracted by detail; can be more pessimistic than optimistic; slow to act.

Lord

Strengths: organised; detailed; analyses every situation; loves research; sees distinctions others miss; able to list out every detail. The Lord's wealth comes from flow – cashflow from leasing assets or, in the case of the Google founders, information flow. Lords love an automated business that never requires them to turn up.

Weaknesses: little patience with social niceties; often involved in excessive organising; can get absorbed in the data; often misses the big picture. Lords act slowly and certainly, which can frustrate those around them.

Mechanic

Strengths: finding a better way of doing something; taking ad hoc ideas and processes (often from Creators) and turning them into repeatable systems or products; able to quickly fine-tune, simplify, replicate and improve; perfectionist and detail-oriented. While Creators are great at starting things, Mechanics are great at finishing things. Their wealth comes from the systems and processes they create – like Ikea founder, Ingvar Kamprad, and Amazon's Jeff Bezos.

Weaknesses: communication style can cause friction; can seem aloof and removed; often very structured and inflexible; focus on perfection can lead to slow willingness to change; may get caught up in the detail.

Which profile are you?

You should have recognised yourself in at least one of the profiles. You can find out for certain which Wealth Profile you are by taking an online test. Find out more about it at ScrewWorkLetsPlay. com/WD.

Hopefully, this has illustrated that the source of your value is far, far broader than the transferable skills you picked up in your last job. Your talents might include inspiring people, encouraging people, driving a bargain, spotting mistakes, connecting people, fine-tuning things, automating, brainstorming. And it also shows that you should stop trying to be an all-rounder once and for all. Work on your strengths, work *around* your weaknesses.

Your mission must be to get into flow: start doing more of those things that you're naturally good at – which are also the things you find most enjoyable. In addition, you will need to *stop* doing those things that are out of flow for you – by delegating them, outsourcing them or swapping skills with complementary people. Few people dare to do this and so most of us never really experience flow. We push and struggle in our work for mediocre results. Imagine only doing the things that you are great at doing and working with others who are great at the things you hate: how much more effective would you be?

Note that there is a world of difference between what you *can* do and what you're naturally great at. Build a life around what you're really talented at and you'll be many times more successful than if you base your work on what you're OK at.

Write in your playbook which profile you think you might be and which strengths you recognise in yourself from the list above. Also write down one thing you currently do in your work that clearly feels *out of flow* for you, something that really grates with you. How could you minimise or remove this activity altogether from your work?

Mike Southon, the beermat entrepreneur

Mike Southon is a serial entrepreneur of 17 start-ups, and co-author of the *Beermat Entrepreneur* series of books. He is now a mentor for other entrepreneurs, and delivers presentations all over the world. He is an expert on Wealth Dynamics.

I asked him for his advice on how to get paid to play.

> *If you team up with a foil, somebody with the opposite set of skills to yourself, you stand much more chance of being able to 'play'. For example, Chris West, my co-author of the 'Beermat' books and I are opposite in every respect; we complement each other. Everything that I am good at, he is bad at, and vice versa. I have a 'Star' profile, while his is 'Mechanic' – this means that I am an extrovert by nature while he is more introverted. We are both very intuitive, but I am better at looking at the big picture, while he has an excellent eye for detail. My idea of 'play' is going out and talking to people, while his idea of 'play' is sitting at home and writing a book.*

> *Chris took all my experiences and turned them into a logical model, which became the basis for our best-selling series of 'Beermat' books. Today, I earn a living as a professional speaker, something I was probably born to do, having had various careers as an actor, stand-up comedian, singer in a band and finally in high-technology sales. Chris earns a living writing books and delivering marketing workshops.*

So my advice to any aspiring entrepreneur is first to understand yourself and psychometric tools such as Wealth Dynamics are very useful for this. Then, you should find a foil, someone who has the opposite and complementary set of skills, as I did with Chris West.

Feeling uncomfortable?

The story of the human race is the story of men and women selling themselves short.

Abraham Maslow, American psychologist, 1908–1970

All this talk of naming your talents and strengths might be unsettling. Perhaps this sounds like boasting to you? British culture in particular has a history of encouraging people not to sing their own praises. But unless you at least identify your talents, how can you ever get to use them? It is a generous act to know your talents and use them. Your talents are not really for you, they are for everyone else around you who benefits when you put them into action. In fact, keeping them to yourself is the selfish act.

It can be easy to overlook something you do well as a talent; it comes so naturally to you, you can't imagine not being able to do it. And you may not have noticed that other people don't have this talent. We're so bought into the idea that what we do for a living must be hard work that getting paid to do what comes naturally almost feels like cheating!

I have a friend who is an excellent flirt. He's genuinely charming and charismatic with everyone he meets. And that's a talent. There are some people who make their entire living teaching other men and women how to flirt. Ask some supportive friends what talents you have that you might have missed and write them down in your playbook.

Talents, skills and passions

The sweet spot for getting paid to play is where talent, skill and passion meet. Talent is what you're born with. Great comedians have been making people laugh since their earliest school days. But when they first step up to a mic to perform they still usually 'die'. This is because pacing, audience interaction and writing material are skills that still have to be learned. The third factor is passion. Even if you're good at something, you won't excel at it unless you enjoy it. I happen to be talented and skilled at wiring extremely complex digital video systems together. It's easy for me and I had a lot of practice in it at a previous job but I'm not passionate about it so there is no way I would make it a central part of my working life.

The fastest route to getting paid to play is to choose something that you are not just talented at and passionate about, but that you already have some knowledge and skills in. Your depth of experience is a large part of how other people value you and decide what to pay you. The problem of course is that when you make a leap into a new field that excites you, you may not have the same level of expertise in it that veterans have. And that can make it difficult to get paid what you would like.

If you choose your steps wisely, you can minimise the setback. The more of the skills you can use from previous work, the quicker you will be able to get paid for the new line of work. Even if you're moving into a completely different field, if you're using the great track record you have built, for example, in managing people or organising projects, you can still be very valuable.

Also think twice before you ditch your previous area of expertise entirely. If you have a talent for something, it may just be the form you use it in your current work that is unsatisfying. I assumed my decades of experience with technology would play no part at all in my new more creative career. But in fact it has become a unique selling point for me when I advise people on internet strategy for their business. My natural affinity for technology hasn't gone away but now I use it in a much more fun way – to find dramatic shortcuts for people to launch their creative projects onto the world. What talents do you have that you could imagine enjoying using if you could just find a more interesting way to employ them? Write them down.

The great love-versus-money balancing act

It's time to make a choice of how to use your mix of talents, skills and passions. If you want to get paid to play, does this mean you have to think commercially about everything you do? In your imagined year off, there are no doubt many different activities you would like to do. Some you want to do purely for love: they seem difficult to monetise or perhaps you don't want to even try. You might not want to expose your most personal creative work to the vagaries of the market – your art, music or poetry for instance. Some of the kinds of work you could imagine doing might be very marketable but perhaps not quite as enjoyable. Which do you choose? This is the eternal love-versus-money balancing act.

The truth is that the 'work you do for money versus work you do for the love of it' dilemma never goes away. Even people who become world famous will continue to manage their careers carefully to balance their most commercial work with their personal passions. Oscar winner George Clooney is pretty much at the top of his game. Like similarly successful actors, however, he will alternate very commercial projects like *Ocean's Eleven* (which grossed $183 million in the US) with ones that are less popular but personally important to him (such as *Syriana* which grossed less than a third as much but won him an Oscar).

For the rest of us, it might mean that, as a writer, you write articles in between books or do commercial copywriting – both of which can be very creative and enjoyable. As a video artist, you fund yourself by shooting corporate videos or adverts. As an internet entrepreneur, you pick up the odd coding job on elance.com to keep yourself going.

Whatever you choose to keep you afloat while you build your more playful life, for heaven's sake make it enjoyable! Don't make the mistake so many make of taking any low-level work no matter how ill-fitting. There are far too many players stuck in boring temp jobs, PA positions, and punishing sales roles. If the work is a terrible fit for you, you'll be so drained afterwards, you'll have no energy for the thing you really want to do. And beware the pitfall of spending months or even years creating some fall-back source of income when you might be better off taking the plunge and starting straight away with what you really want to do.

Your aim is to find a mix of work – some more like play than others, some more financially rewarding than others – but none of it that is too far from playing. Make sure you are in *flow*, doing something that gives you some of the experience of what you truly love. Get it right and you might find your more commercial work becoming symbiotic with the work you do purely for pleasure.

Getting paid to watch YouTube

Lindsey Mountford has always known she wanted to write books but, after finishing her English literature degree with a heap of debt, she needed a job. She fell into media sales and a series of mostly miserable jobs that involved 'getting on the phone by 9am, selling classified ad space to jaded, angry media buyers'.

She was soon sick of it,

but then I got promoted, got more money. I left to sell online advertising for another company, chasing the money. This happened a couple of times as I always got bored too quickly. I had the feeling 99% of the people I worked with hated their jobs too. We all wasted an awful lot of time emailing friends, chatting on MSN, being on Facebook when we should have been working. I felt like I was selling my soul but I still had no idea of any other career I could go into.

Finally I came to work for a small start-up company that runs the website viralvideochart.com and also distributes videos around the web, giving them the best chance of 'going viral.' I have to know about viral marketing and all the latest trends in social media so now I get paid to spend time on YouTube, Twitter, Facebook and blogs! My clients are genuinely interested in what we have to say, my ideas are listened to, and I feel like I'm engaging my brain.

Working here is an absolute blast – the people here are enthusiastic, intelligent and I really respect and admire them. The videos we deal with are always original, random, funny. They're for so many different kinds of companies and I'm so busy that there's no time to get bored. We don't have the culture of staying really late after work, so I can be home by 7pm to start writing and I don't feel like I've been frying my brains all day with boring work; in fact I'm often inspired by things I have to watch on YouTube as part of my job.

The job has actually helped my writing in a lot of ways. I need a lot of structure in my day, with too much free time I end up doing nothing so work is the framework I can be creative in. I feel settled and happy in my job, so for the first time in my life I'm not spending all my spare time worrying about my career. Not having to worry about money anymore has really 'set me free' creatively.

Now I've finished the first draft of my book and I'm onto editing it. Things that I think about at work (like digital news reporting and the viral spread of ideas) have hugely influenced the story. In fact, the main idea in my novel is the spread of a fake story in the press which goes viral and has a huge impact, inadvertently sparking off global mass hysteria.

How to avoid being a starving artist (or actor or musician or poet or novelist . . .)

If you're passionate about your art, acting, music, poetry or novel writing, you'll already be well aware of the difficulties of making a living from them. The cold, hard reality of the creative arts is that there is plenty of supply (i.e. people wanting to create) and not a huge amount of demand (people willing to pay money for what you create). This makes the arts very competitive. As a result it's a challenge to succeed but, hey, it's a challenge to do anything really important.

You want to keep doing your art and you don't want to starve. What can you do? First off, quit the dilemma once and for all of asking 'Can I continue my art?' You *are* an artist; you don't get to choose. The question now is '*How* do I continue my art?' What do you need to do in order to be able to create your art and make a living – even if the two things have to be separate at first? Think about how you will manage the development of your art over time. Let go of the idea that the choice is either to be a full-time artist or to give up. Manage your love-versus-money balance to make it work.

If you're serious about making a full-time living from your art, decide that you will do whatever it takes to make it happen. Get creative about what you produce and how you market it. If the conventions of your field are working against you, sidestep them. Model the people you respect who have succeeded in your field. Everyone says acting is very hard to make a living out of, yet some actors always have work (and they're not necessarily the most talented). How do they do it? What can you learn from them?

Get over the idea that if you just produce good work, you will magically be discovered. Realise that to make any progress, you need to put at least as much effort into promoting your work as you do making it. If you're terrible at self-promotion, find someone else to do it for you. You can sit in a garret painting for the rest of your life but if you never tell anyone about your work, no one will ever get to enjoy it. It's remarkable the number of people I see writing music or novels who never dare show it to anyone. The creative act is incomplete without an audience. Yes, it's frightening to share your creative work and hear what could be negative feedback but don't you dare use that as a reason to avoid it!

What's the worst that could happen? Someone might say that all your work to date is utterly worthless. They could even be right. And still, you would be an artist. It might be that you haven't found the right medium for yourself yet. Whatever it is you're trying to express through your art is still valid. Perhaps you shouldn't even be painting, you should be writing. Or if you're writing, you should be painting. Perhaps you haven't dared to go deep enough into what you're trying to express. The only thing you can do wrong is to give up the whole game.

The facts are always friendly.

Carl Rogers, American psychologist and researcher

Embrace portfolio working; don't waste any energy on complaining; take responsibility for your own success and learn from successful artists how to make it work.

How to choose what to do next

So now you have some idea of how valuable your talents can be, what do you do with them? You might have several options in mind for where to head next, but how do you choose the right one to pursue now? Or maybe you can't seem to come up with a single viable path to take? Perhaps you've been thinking about all this for a while now. If you've been going round in circles trying to decide on your next move, you are probably stuck in 'pinball thinking'.

Here's a pattern I see a lot in the participants in careers workshops. The career-changer is stuck in a job they don't enjoy but can't seem to find a new direction to move in. They are longing for someone else to tell them the magic answer of what work they should do. They believe the answer is *out there somewhere* – some job option they haven't thought of yet. And once someone shows them it, everything will drop into place.

Does this sound familiar to you? In reality, the information is within you; you've simply discounted too many options by getting into 'pinball thinking'. Just like the ball-bearing in a game of pinball, your internal dialogue about possible work options rapidly pings back and forth before falling down a hole. Does the conversation in your head sound something like the following?

I know, I could be a writer!

Oh no, I couldn't stand the isolation.

Maybe I could start my own business!

But it's too risky right now to do that.

I could try PR.

But I'd have to retrain and I don't have the money.

Ah, I'm stuck . . .

I have no idea what I want to do.

(Game over)

In reality, of course, you've had three ideas just in that one internal conversation. In each one of those ideas there is something that speaks to you. That means there is information there about the kind of work you find attractive: information that you're currently discarding.

Here's a better way of thinking. Take all your ideas for possible directions for your work, as flawed as they may be, and get them down on paper. To help with this, look back at the notes in your playbook from Secret one: the activities you would do in a year out, the things you enjoyed most in your career, the people you admire or are jealous of, the projects you would do if you couldn't fail, and the things you enjoy so much you find it difficult to stop doing them. All these answers point to what you want more of in your working life. Make a list of work options – careers, jobs, freelance roles, business ideas, or creative projects – that will give you something of the experience you really want.

If some of the activities you originally wrote down seem impossible right now (renovating a castle, sailing around the world, studying yoga in India for six months), don't throw them out just yet. This is telling you about something that you want more of in your life. What is it? Is it freedom, adventure, personal development, working in a team, having an impact on the world? Is it the experience of working with your hands, creating something new, improving something, solving a tough problem, realising a vision? What kind of work could give you some of this? Remember there is always a way to get the experience you want to have, even if it's in a different form to what you first thought of.

Write down at least three to five work options. Include the kind of work you currently do, just for comparison. Then for each option write answers to the following four questions:

➡ What is it that *appeals* about this job, business or project?

➡ What is it that's *unattractive* to me and doesn't appeal about this option?

➡ What are the practical obstacles that might get in the way of taking this option?

➡ What *assets* do I have in my favour for this option? Talents, skills, knowledge, experience, contacts?

So for the example option of writing a book, you might write:

Appeals: being creative; getting my ideas out into the world; having an impact; becoming famous!

Doesn't appeal: doesn't pay very well; I might not be self-disciplined enough to write a whole book on my own.

Obstacles: I don't know anyone who could get me published; my spelling is really bad.

Assets: I've written a couple of articles and people have said they're good; I really enjoy putting my ideas down on paper; my friend knows a literary agent; I think I've got a good topic.

Then repeat this process for at least a couple of other options, writing out the answers to the four questions for each one.

Now you've got all your imperfect options laid out in front of you, instead of throwing them away, you can start to address the problem areas. How could you minimise the part of this option that doesn't appeal? For the writing example, perhaps you could co-write something or create your book by transcribing talks to an audience.

Then look at the obstacles and brainstorm ways around them. In the writing example, who do you know who could put you in contact with someone in the publishing world? Is there an event you could go to where you could meet a publisher? Could you use spell-check software to get round your problem with spelling?

When you've worked on all the downsides of each option, take a fresh look at the list. Even if you still have practical concerns, which one of these options is most exciting to you? What's the part that's most exciting about it? How can you have that exciting part, while minimising the unappealing part and sidestepping the obstacles? Remember from the last chapter that there is always a way to have the part you want most – even if you have to use some seriously lateral thinking to find a way to get it.

Now look at the common themes emerging in the 'What appeals about this' column. What does this tell you about the kind of work that is attractive to you right now? Are there other ways you could get this appealing part? As you think of more options to explore, add them to your notes. Is there some way to combine several of your desirable options into a new one? If so, put that new option down. Come back to your notes over the next few days and weeks and add new ideas as they come to you. Don't try and work it all out in one sitting.

You can download editable worksheets to fill in for this exercise from ScrewWorkLetsPlay.com

Which of these options do you want to investigate first? You're not committing to changing your whole career, you're just choosing which to look into a bit more deeply. Mark your two or three favourite options. You can research all of them but for now, pick one of these favourites to look at first.

As a player, there really is no single career that is the ultimate answer for you; your career is something you play out by testing, exploring, experimenting and experiencing. As you get clearer and clearer where you want to head next, you adjust your course to move closer to getting paid to play.

Take the Sunday Night Test

It's important to check that the path you're choosing to explore further is something you are genuinely interested in and you're not just following the expectations that others have of you. Imagine it's Sunday night. Tomorrow, Monday morning, you are starting this new work life you have chosen from your list. How do you feel? Are you excited? Maybe a little bit scared? Good! Or are you just feeling flat, resigned? Change the details of this option until you can imagine looking forward to doing it.

If all else fails, toss a coin. If you can't decide between two or more directions you could choose, try tossing a coin. At the moment you discover the result, check in quickly with how you feel – are you secretly a little bit disappointed or a little bit excited? Find a way to do the one that excites you.

If you're still stuck, choose anything on the list. If you've been stuck in the grip of a career crisis for some time, it's common to end up in a state of mild to moderate depression (even if you haven't identified it as such yet). This is not a very resourceful state for building a new life. So choosing to engage in anything you enjoy is a good thing to do. It makes you a little happier and it reconnects you with your passion and creativity. And you need these to make changes in your life. That's why people often find doing something enjoyable but quite unrelated to their work (e.g. joining a choir, starting an evening class) seems to unlock them and enable them to move on.

In the next chapter you will find out how to get started right away on exploring one of the options on your list.

Put it into play

Keys to this secret:

➡ Get into flow; maximise your moment of magic, work on your strengths, work around your weaknesses. This will bring you far greater success in much less time.

➡ Get others to tell you strengths you might be taking for granted.

➡ Stop pinball thinking and lay out all your options to assess.

What you should have now:

➡ an idea of your moment of magic; the strengths used and the impact it has on others;

➡ some idea of what being in flow looks like for you;

➡ a shortlist of options to investigate further and a favourite to start with.

Take ten minutes to play:

➡ Go and experience your moment of magic! Find a way to do that thing you're naturally good at which people get a lot of value from. Call someone up now and offer to do this for free for them if necessary.

Exclusive extras on ScrewWorkLetsPlay.com

➡ more information on Wealth Dynamics and how to take the test;

➡ editable worksheets for you to download and fill in to solve your pinball thinking and choose what to do next.

Secret three
How to get started right now

There are no rules or formulas for success. You just have to live it and do it. Knowing this gives us enormous freedom to experiment toward what we want. Believe me, it's a crazy, complicated journey. It's trial and error. It's opportunism. It's quite literally, 'Let's try lots of this stuff and see how it works.'

Dame Anita Roddick 1942–2007, founder of The Body Shop

You should now have some idea of the talents you have to offer and a shortlist of options of how to put them to use. In this chapter we'll look at how to put it all into action right away and launch your journey to get paid to play. In order to do that, you'll need to embrace a new, more playful way of approaching work that does away with five-year plans and long-term goals. If you can do that, you might be surprised – and delighted – just where your work ends up taking you, as young entrepreneurs Sam Bompas and Harry Parr have discovered.

Playing with food

Sam Bompas and Harry Parr set up their company Bompas & Parr a couple of years ago to enable them to do fun experiments with food. Since then, they've engaged the world's greatest architects to design jellies for them to make, they've run a scratch and sniff cinema screening, and they've created the first breathable gin and tonic.

As Harry explains,

One of the first projects came about with a phone call from Warwick Castle asking to make a giant model of the castle out of jelly. We realised that what they wanted was actually impossible so Sam somehow decided that what they really wanted was a 12 course Victorian breakfast and not this giant jelly. And amazingly they decided to commission this breakfast. So we went from a project about jelly to being commissioned to do an elaborate 12 course feast. We had pitched the food that they served to Queen Victoria when she was at the castle. So, we thought 'Well how are we going to do this and pull it all together?' And at the time I was training to become an architect so I thought the only way to do it was just to draw a plan. So we went down into the utmost detail about how everything was going to be served and we ended up doing choreography for all of the servants so that every part of the meal could be served at exactly the right time.

And then we instructed our friends, who we dressed up as Victorian servants and butlers, that as long as they followed exactly what was on this little drawing that we had, that everything would be fine. And it all worked out really well at the end.

And that's when we realised that we could pitch just about anything and work out quite quickly afterwards how we're going to do it. We can always make it work by the time it all happens.

Find out more about Sam & Harry's projects at *jellymongers.co.uk*

Most of the players I have interviewed, including Bompas and Parr, are fully engaged in an exciting process of playing out their work but couldn't say where it will take them in five years' time. This is a very different approach to careers to what most of us have been taught.

Myth 6: I can't start anything until I know exactly where I'm heading

Today, there is little point picking some goal far off in the distance and expecting to be able to follow a well-planned path to get you there – things are moving too damn fast and life never turns out the way you expect it to anyway. Aside from that, each step you take positions you at a different place with a different view and different choices. There's no way to predict in advance what opportunities will present themselves and how you'll feel about them once you're there. Better to play it out; choose your next step because you really want to do it for its own merits – even if you can't see how it might fit with your career or some master plan to make you rich.

As my friend, Mark, said when he saw me reading a careers book, 'Why do you bother? Don't worry about a "career", just pick an interesting project and go do it. And when you've done that one, see where it's landed you and pick the next one.' This process has led to him becoming an expert in his field (teaching English as a foreign language) and travelling all over the world with his work. He's currently in Vietnam setting up his own English school.

Beware the 'good career move' or the business chosen purely for the financial rewards. This is not the route to a happy life. Billionaire Warren Buffett was once asked for careers advice by an MBA student. The student thought he should go work in finance for a while just to make money then do what he really wanted to later. The billionaire thought this was a ridiculous idea, and said, 'That's like saving sex for old age.' Besides, it's very difficult to get rich by doing something you don't enjoy. You can't really excel at something when your heart isn't in it.

Two of my best career moves were instinctual and turned out very well. Straight out of college, I joined a tiny software start-up of three people which went on to become one of the best-known names in their industry, creating systems to automate TV stations all over the world. Then I moved to a small start-up making special effects software. The week I joined they were bought by the biggest name in the business. This led to me having an extremely impressive CV without any deliberate planning.

So was I just lucky? Perhaps not. Even if I couldn't describe my criteria at the time, I was joining early-stage companies with smart people doing very original work. And smart people doing very original work often go on to become industry-leading companies (or get bought by them). When later I joined a 'Big 5' consultancy because it seemed a 'good career move', I gained an impressive job title but I was miserable.

If you pursue the projects that you enjoy and that feel important to you, it's more likely to lead to success and financial riches than plotting for some far-off end goal and making compromising 'good career moves' along the way.

The problem with goals

But shouldn't you at least set some goals? If you've ever worked with a coach or read a book about success, you've probably been advised to set goals. Well, if goals were so powerful, a lot more people would reach them – and everyone who did would be happy. There are a number of problems with this incessant goal setting. It places a focus on the future and suggests relentless action and compromise in the present to get there. When you achieve that goal, you allow yourself a brief period of rejoicing and then set a new one. Ugh! I can feel the existential desolation just writing that. It's all very mesomorphic, by which I mean action-focused.

What about how you want to be or *feel* from moment to moment? There's no goal you can tick off for that.

Myth 7: Once my life is the way I want it to be, then I'll be happy

Your goals won't make you happy. The truth is it's not anything in the future that will make you happy but how you live *today*, how you choose to create this day of your life. Even getting rich is no guarantee of happiness. Research shows that when people win the lottery, they have a short-lived boost in happiness and then settle back to roughly the level of happiness they had before.

It's not your success that will create your happiness. It's your happiness that will create your success. And you can't create happiness in the future by consistently creating misery in your life now. If you can't create what you want in some form today, it's likely you will never have it. I'm sure you've seen the kind of person who is always running faster and faster in the hope of creating a more relaxed future and of course never gets there.

> *Most people treat the present moment as if it were an obstacle that they need to overcome. Since the present moment is Life itself, it is an insane way to live.*
>
> **Eckhart Tolle, author of *The Power Of Now***

The healthier alternative is to create a good present that grows into a great future. Turn your focus from far-off goals to the present day and create some of the experience of your dream life in the here and now – even if it's scaled down to start with. Play out the unfolding of your life's work; pick a project that will give you more of what you want – and start it right away.

When you focus on getting into flow today – doing what you enjoy and what comes naturally to you – you'll be amazed just how fast you'll find yourself progressing.

The problem with thinking

Thinking is overrated. And most of us do far too much of it. Successful people apparently have fewer thoughts; they don't engage in endless deliberation. Perhaps this is because the research shows that over-thinking makes you miserable and unmotivated.

Over thinking (i.e., rumination) ushers in a host of adverse consequences: It sustains or worsens sadness, fosters negatively-biased thinking, impairs a person's ability to solve problems, saps motivation, and interferes with concentration and initiative.

Sonja Lyubomirsky, *The How Of Happiness*

If you're truly stuck in your life and can't seem to move forward, chances are you're thinking too much. A lot of people who turn up at careers workshops are stuck in the thinking trap. I know it well: I've wasted years there myself. It's the belief that if we sit and think about something for long enough, the light will shine down from above and we'll find some new answer not available to us before. Unfortunately, this very rarely happens. Why do we even think it would? If you've thought about a problem for five minutes and not found the solution, more time spent sitting alone thinking without any new input is very unlikely to bring fresh insights.

I guess it's school that taught us that thinking was the solution – if you don't have the answer at first, think harder. This might work for a maths problem but it doesn't work very well for life decisions. The problem is that we think within our own limits of what we know and what we believe is possible. Career problems are very rarely problems of external limitation; they are more usually a reflection of the limits of our knowledge and beliefs.

The solution? Stop thinking and start playing. Here's how to do it.

Pick a play project

It's time to stop trying to find the perfect answer for what to do with your life, and start today doing something you really want to do. Look at the shortlist of options you produced in the last chapter and the one that you marked out as most exciting to investigate first.

What small project could you start straight away that will launch you into this line of work, or at least allow you to try it out? This is your first play project. It should be something you can do in a few weeks or a couple of months. You may have already had a taste of this activity in your first experiment with Play Wednesday as explained in Secret one. The point now is to define something that will give you a tangible result and with a clear end point. If this is a new activity for you and you're not sure how much you'll enjoy it, choose something small enough that you can finish before you get bored. Break it down if it's currently too large.

'Find a happy person, and you will find a project.'

Happiness researcher Sonja Lyubomirsky writes in her book *The How of Happiness*: 'People who strive for something significant, whether it's learning a new craft or raising moral children, are far happier than those who don't have strong dreams or aspirations. Find a happy person and you will find a project.'

The content of your project will depend on what stage you are at in your search. If you're still weighing up possible options, your project should help you explore and experience this option. If you've already got some idea where you want to head, this project should launch you right into doing it.

Philip's first play project was to sell one of his inventions for the first time. For Juliette, it was to write a book proposal (which then turned into a website, freshairfix.com). For freelance marketing consultant Karen, it was developing her writing and her ideas in a blog. For Roshini, it was to experiment with drawing comics.

How to choose your project

Don't obsess about what project you should do. It doesn't have to represent the future direction of your entire life, it's simply to give you an experience of one of the options you chose in the last chapter. The point is to get into motion. You can always correct your course on the fly. If it's something that calls to you right now and you think you'd enjoy doing it, go for it. If it will take you somewhere interesting or you will learn something in the process that will be useful to you for subsequent projects, then all the better. Whatever you choose, you're likely to learn reusable skills even if your next project is completely different – skills such as how to ask people for help, how to collaborate, how to keep going when you feel stuck and how to manage your motivation, creativity and time. You'll also get to experience your own ability to manifest something that you want in your life. This is a wonderful thing in itself if you've been feeling powerless about improving your work situation.

Make sure to choose something that is likely to be enjoyable to do, not just for the result. The bottom line is if it didn't give you the results you hoped for and doesn't make you rich, would you still be glad you did it? Aim for a project that will give you an experience of being in flow, perhaps centred on something you know is a moment of magic for you. But bear in mind that the best projects are a step up for you and might be a bit scary to take on. We'll see later how to manage your anxiety about taking on new challenges.

The project you choose will depend on where you are right now in your shift from worker to player. Here are three specific options for common situations.

If you're in career paralysis

If you've got completely stuck on what to do with your career, almost any project you feel excited about will have the benefit of getting you moving again. Don't worry too much about how it might lead to making a living. You can focus on making money or progressing your move with later projects (Secret five will help you with this). The main thing for you is to get into play and indulge yourself by becoming immersed in something you'll really enjoy.

I meet people all the time who long to be, for example, a writer but have been deliberating whether it's possible for them. If you want to be a writer, grab a pen and paper and start writing. Congratulations, you're now a writer! If you've been dabbling with writing for a while now, make your project to enter a writing competition, or to write an article to get published on a website. Even if you don't end up making a career out of writing, you will have had the experience of doing it and will have learned what that's like for you. You'll probably also have come up with a few new ideas of what to try next.

If you're self-employed

If you're already self-employed, use your project to open up a new line of business that's closer to your heart, that keeps you in flow, and that feels more like play. Think about the pieces of work you have done in the past that you have most enjoyed. How could you run a campaign to focus on winning more of exactly that kind of work now? It's surprising how few people do this! You could also use your play project to open another channel of contact with your target market such as writing a blog, using social media, or starting a live event. Or you might use it as your first foray into passive income and try out making money without turning up (more on this later).

If you're moving into a completely new field

If you're looking to enter a completely new line of work, use your project as a chance to immerse yourself in it and start exploring. Here's how.

1. Start to live this new line of work. Read books about it and autobiographies of leaders in this field. Read magazines and watch DVDs about the topic; go to exhibitions.
2. Get in the mix. Go out to networking meetings, talks and workshops. Talk to others and learn what's hot in this part of the world.
3. Take any chance you can to experience doing the kind of work you're interested in, even if unpaid to start with.

Once you know the field you want to enter, if you're aiming to land a job rather than go self-employed, choose a play project that could get you noticed by possible employers: interview thought leaders in this area and write an article on what you find out, or help out at an exhibition or conference.

Even faster than Google

> **Myth 8: I should go and research this all day on the internet**
>
> You might be thinking that the best way to find out about a new field you want to work in is to go and research it thoroughly on the internet. A certain amount of reading around is important but beware of getting drawn into an endless process of research sitting at your computer. It's a huge time-sink and doesn't really show you what it's like to work in this field. Career decisions ultimately cannot be made with rational thinking alone, they must *feel* right – and research will only take you so far.

▶

> Beware in particular using 'research' as a way to systematically discount the career paths you are really excited about. If you go looking for evidence that something is impossible, you'll find it.

Once you've researched the basics, here's something even faster than Google. Think of a key question you need the answer to – something that could move you forward significantly. Then find someone who could answer it for you: someone who is actually doing the kind of work you're interested in. Try to choose someone who is successful at it and enjoys it. You'll be amazed just what you can find out in ten minutes speaking to someone knowledgeable. Most people will be quite happy to help you by talking about their work for ten minutes.

Here's how to approach it.

➡ Decide what's the one question you would most like an answer to right now. Be specific so it's easy to answer. Don't ask, 'What's llama farming like?' Say 'I want to get into llama farming, can you tell me what your typical day consists of?' Don't ask the basic stuff you can find on the internet, focus on asking about the things that come from real-world experience.

➡ Who do you know who might be able to answer your question? If you can't think of anyone, who do you know that might know someone who can? We all know as many as 200 people. By asking friends to ask their friends and colleagues, you immediately access 40,000 people.

Use what you find out in your ongoing research and when you're ready, think of your next question to ask.

Wanted: chemical explosives expert

Sam Bompas of Bompas & Parr told me that in one of their most recent projects,

> We created a breathable cocktail. We vaporised gin and tonic to make a cocktail cloud that filled a building. If you're in there for 40 minutes you have the equivalent of a strong G&T.

This project had considerable health and safety risks:

> If you vaporise spirits the resulting fog is extremely flammable. We got in touch with a leading chemical explosives expert and asked him to get involved with the project. We didn't have any budget for consultancy work but he thought it sounded like fun and answered our question 'How much alcohol can you vaporise before it becomes an explosive risk?'

> If you put the hours in you're going to be able to speak to the right person. You can always find people that know more than you. You just need to track them down.

Think big, start small

Have you got a grand vision for a business or a creative project? The key is to break it down into something small enough to be manageable. Here are some quickfire examples.

If you want to a write a book, you could start writing your ideas out as a blog and assemble them later into a book. I started writing a blog to experiment with my ideas about getting paid to play and this led to the book you're reading right now. If you want to write a novel, start with a short story, or write an outline of your novel ready to show to a more experienced novelist and get feedback.

Want to write an album? Make it your play project to create one track good enough to play to a friend. Then create two more and you have a single. Put it on MySpace. Seven more tracks and you have an album. Sell it using one of the dozens of services on the web designed for the purpose.

If you want to start a business, you could start by exploring the idea or the brand on the web – blog about it, assemble images in a tumblelog (a simple form of blog), twitter your findings 140 characters at a time. You'll be able to play out your idea, get feedback, attract collaborators and at the same time you'll be building followers who later could become paying customers or clients. Or you could sketch out the proposition, then go find a test customer and win your first *playcheque*. More on this later.

If you want to sell goods or trade international crafts, start on eBay, move on to your own eBay shop and then graduate to your own website. If you're making your own handmade crafts, go to etsy.com or similar site to sell them.

If you already have your own business but want to nudge it towards something that feels more playful to you, choose a project that will explore a new, more enjoyable, income stream. Look for that sweet spot of doing something you really enjoy which fulfils a need your customers already have. You'll know when you're on track as you'll find you attract interest quickly.

Artists, turn your home into a gallery. Julian Bolt from London is a great photographer but prone to getting creatively blocked. With encouragement from his creativity group and his wife Sonia, he decided to hold the first exhibition of his work. Since he didn't have access to a gallery he held it in his small basement flat in an unfashionable part of London. He and Sonia stayed up late for many nights, clearing up the flat, printing his images and mounting them on the walls. He received plenty of positive feedback from the constant stream of visitors and sold nearly £3,000 of photos. One of the visitors was a gallery owner. She agreed to give Julian his own exhibition in her beautiful art gallery in the heart of London's gallery quarter. His next exhibition after that was in a Parisian gallery.

Want to launch a regular event? I run a monthly London event called Scanners Night for creative people who want to do lots of different projects. I often get requests from people asking me if I can run one near them somewhere in the UK or elsewhere in the world. Although we are considering taking Scanners Night national, until we do, I give the following advice on how to start your own; it's exactly what I did when I started. Put a notice on a bulletin board where the people you want to invite hang out and also put a listing on Meetup.com or craigslist. Invite people to meet in a pub or café to chat. You might base it around a particular topic of discussion or give a brief talk yourself, or meet at an interesting exhibition. If you're worried you might be sitting on your own all night, call a couple of friends to come along. The worst-case scenario then is that you spend a pleasant night talking with your friends. Grow it into a regular event that you could eventually start charging people to attend.

Want to change the world? Take a tip from Mohammed Yunus, creator of the Grameen Bank which pioneered microloans to some of the poorest people in the world. In 1976 Professor Yunus loaned $27 out of his own pocket to 42 women in a village in Bangladesh. The women were making furniture and were forced to pay all their profits to loan sharks for the bamboo they used as raw material. The tiny sum allowed the women to pay off the loans and start to pull themselves out of poverty. Today Grameen Bank has over 7 million borrowers and has loaned over $6 billion with a 98 per cent recovery rate. Yunus and the Grameen Bank were awarded the Nobel Peace Prize in 2006.

What can you do as a project in just a few weeks that will set you on the path to your grand vision? Using the above examples as inspiration, write down your larger objective and then sketch out a small project that allows you to take your first step.

Some of my entrepreneurial clients hate the idea of starting their business in this incremental way. They believe they should go for the big splash and launch with a fabulous website and branding from day one.

This is OK if you have a couple of successful ventures under your belt already or you have the money to do formal market research but it's a bad idea for those of us just starting out. Why? Right now as you begin your business or creative project, you think you know what it's going to be, but the truth is you don't. As soon as it's exposed to the atmosphere, it changes. When you put your idea out into the world, it morphs and evolves as you interact with the potential market or audience; it must if you want to create something successful.

Even if you happen to have a great idea, you might not realise where the real value is in it. You might design a brand at an early stage that's all about how your product has a cool design but you might discover that people buy it because it saves them the expense of buying a higher priced alternative. Even big companies get it wrong sometimes. When the mobile networks enabled text messaging, they expected it to be used simply as a replacement for a pager but text messages now outnumber calls and account for over $50 billion of annual revenue.

Get your idea out there and evolve it on the fly.

Kick off your play project

Begin somewhere; you cannot build a reputation on what you intend to do.

Liz Smith, columnist

Start on your project as soon as you can. Why not now? Even if you only have ten minutes right now, feeling you've made a start will make a big difference to your motivation. If you have no time now, take out your diary and make an appointment with yourself in the next few days to start (we'll look more at managing your time in the next chapter). When you're ready, ask yourself what task you could do in the time you have available that would make the biggest impact on your project and begin it.

Use Play Wednesday as a day to carve out some time for your play project and start to move your working week a little closer to your vision of a year out. Having set days or times when you work on your play project also makes it far more likely you will make a habit of it.

Commit to your play project. Don't just dabble. Have you got into the habit of fiddling with lots of things but dropping them before they reach a conclusion and before anyone else gets to benefit from them? The creative act is incomplete without an audience. How many pieces of writing sit languishing in drawers? How many songs remain only in the singer's head? How many business ideas have never been shared for fear of someone stealing them? Don't be one of those that as Henry David Thoreau said, 'go to the grave with the song still in them'.

Follow through on your project until it's done. Create something tangible and share it with the world. The sharing could be as simple as playing your finished music to a friend, putting your short story on a website somewhere, talking your initial business idea over with an expert, or emailing the description of your ideal job to everyone you know.

When you're not used to finishing things, you may not realise how much there is to learn by doing so. That last 10 per cent you need to do to finish your project is actually 50 per cent of the work. At the point you realise you are going to share the output of your project, you are forced to round off the rough edges and make sure it's in a form that others will appreciate. It's also in the sharing that much of the learning takes place – you have to marshal your nerves to make your work public and dare to hear the feedback.

Decide how you will share the results of your project and set a date to do it. Write this down now in your diary as your *release date*. Also put it some place you will see it every day so you don't forget. Then arrange this date in advance. Let the people you'll be sharing your project with know now. This will help keep you focused. You can always renegotiate it if you absolutely have to.

Plan now how you will celebrate reaching your release date and completing your project. If you march on without acknowledging what you've done, you reduce your motivation for reaching your release date next time around. What will you do to treat yourself? Take a day off, go for a celebratory meal, treat yourself to a massage, or buy some gadget you've been longing to own? Write this in your diary next to your release date.

For some projects, it is not possible to predict when you will complete it; for instance, winning your first piece of self-employed work. You can still get clear in advance though how you will celebrate it and it can be useful to estimate how long you expect it to take.

The benefits of being in play

When you finally stop sitting around thinking and get into motion, wonderful things happen. Firstly, you get lots of feedback – both internal and external. The external feedback is about what you're good at and what you're not so good at. The internal feedback is how it felt, what you enjoyed and what you didn't. Record it all in your playbook.

The other thing is that once you're in motion, the view is completely different. Just like the view is different for the person who gets on the train compared to the person who stays behind on the platform. In transit, all sorts of opportunities present themselves that aren't visible when you're sitting at home researching on Google. You run into people who can help you on your project; you get recommendations for books you can read and websites you can use, and people ask you to help them with their projects. You might even make some money or get a job offer before you've really tried to!

Having a project you're committed to gives you definition, direction, a mission. And having a mission is attractive. Like me, you've probably met people who say, 'Well, I'd quite like to do x but then again I also might do y'. Your attitude towards them is very different from that with someone who says, 'I'm creating this event that's happening in a month's time'. You're much more likely to be able to offer helpful contacts or advice to the latter person. The clearer the purpose of your project and the more committed you are to it, the more you'll find that people step forward to help you.

Remember, when you find yourself in a café enjoying writing or you have a moment when you know you've really enjoyed helping someone, or when you've created a piece of code that works like a charm and people are using it live on the web, take a moment to appreciate it. Because as soon as you are in play, you've already arrived. You've created some of the life you wanted. Yes, it might be making you very little or no money; yes, it might not be the perfect experience; yes, it might have been a stressful ride to get here. Put the 'buts' aside for a moment and appreciate what you do have. It might take a while before your play turns into something that makes you money or gives you the status you'd like, but if you're having fun along the way, you will at least be enjoying the journey.

A moment of play

When I very first escaped the world of jobs and went freelance, I approached a company who were doing very cool work in music software. They hired me to write a program for an exhibit to be placed in the prestigious London Science Museum. I cycled across town to meet them at their office: a converted warehouse on the South Bank of the River Thames. The founder greeted me warmly at the door and led me into a workspace packed with elaborate electronic instruments.

We sat down with a coffee and talked over how we could represent digital sound in a way that even children at a museum could grasp. We talked about waveforms and physics and brainstormed funky ways of displaying it all. When we'd finished, I left and cycled along the South Bank just as the sun was beginning to set over St Paul's Cathedral. I realised that this was an important moment representing the life I had always wanted; I was no longer working, I was playing.

Now imagine this: what if everyone stopped waiting and hoping for their dreams to come true and simply started a project that will get them a little closer to living their dream life in the here and now? Wouldn't that be a better world to live in?

In the next chapter you'll find out how to cope with the ups and downs of getting paid to play and how you can guarantee that you get there in the end.

Put it into play

Keys to this secret:

➡ Don't worry about career plans and long-term goals; play out your unfolding work direction.

➡ Choose a project to try out your favourite work option from the last chapter and start it straight away.

➡ Whatever grand vision you may have, find a way to break it down into something you can start now.

➡ Set a release date for your project, decide how you will share the results with others, and plan to celebrate when you get there!

What you should have now:

➡ a play project defined and a release date.

Take ten minutes to play:

➡ Start right now. Put the book down, and take ten minutes to start on your play project. Whatever your project is, you'll be surprised what you can achieve in ten focused, uninterrupted minutes. Grab the nearest piece of paper and sketch out your idea, or start writing, or go register for a blog, or call someone who can help you.

Exclusive extras on ScrewWorkLetsPlay.com

➡ recordings of interviews with Sam and Harry of Bompas & Parr talking about how they started their remarkable business around food.

Secret four
How to guarantee your success

Life is an ongoing process of choosing between safety (out of fear and need for defence) and risk (for the sake of progress and growth). Make the growth choice a dozen times a day.

Abraham Maslow, American psychologist, 1908–1970

You've now seen how to start a project that will take you one step closer to getting paid to play. Hopefully you've also taken a few minutes to actually begin it. Now let's make this really clear: there is always a way to get the experience you really want in your work. If you're flexible about how you get it, and you're willing to start working on it without knowing exactly where you're heading, you are guaranteed to get it if you simply don't stop.

Making tea for the bailiffs

Twenty-six years ago Leslie Scott borrowed her baby brother's wooden bricks and invented a game with them. She built a tower of bricks and challenged friends to remove blocks without collapsing the tower. People loved playing her simple game and when she left her job in marketing, she decided to get some of them manufactured to sell, calling the game 'Jenga'.

In the early stages of running her business to launch the game, she ran into considerable debt. She reports that one day 'This chap turned up, knocked on the door, and explained that I hadn't kept up with the payments on the car so he'd come to take it away. My attitude at the time was something like "Oh dear, I quite liked that car, but I can live without it". He was quite surprised when I invited him in and said, "Come and have a cup of tea before you take it away".'

Leslie survived the debt and the bailiffs and after several years signed a deal with Hasbro, a multinational toy manufacturer. Jenga has now sold 50 million units and has become the second biggest-selling game in the world, topped only by Monopoly.

Leslie told me that 'People ask me all the time "Were you surprised Jenga became so big?" and I know they expect me to say "Yes", but the honest truth is that I had assumed from the outset that the game would be big. I would say that that's what defines an entrepreneur – you're prepared to take incredible risks because you believe that you are backing a winner.'

Welcome to the roller-coaster

Fasten your seatbelt because you're going on a roller-coaster ride. Once you set off on this journey it is far from smooth running. When you finally dare to admit what you really want and go after it, you will be giving up the constant flat line of mild discontent so many people spend their lives in. You will be *living*, not just existing. You will have fantastic highs as you achieve something you didn't even think possible. And you'll also have real lows when you get a big setback, someone important rejects your idea or says something very critical.

If you're used to living by the adage, 'Don't get your hopes up', I invite you to do the opposite. *Do* get your hopes up; dare to dream that you can have what you want. And, yes, if you hit a big setback, it will hurt. This is normal. Take a moment to lick your wounds, commiserate with friends, then keep on marching. There's always another way to get the experience you really want. In fact, these setbacks are your friends. Most people give up at the first obstacle and that means less competition for you. The only thing you can do wrong is to stop.

Having positive expectations has been shown in most situations to bring better results than expecting the worst. It's no coincidence that most successful entrepreneurs are optimists. And it's also suggested that appreciating what's already working in your life has greater benefits than obsessing about what's not working. This idea has received a lot of airplay recently from believers in the law of attraction but is this really a law of physics or just wishful thinking?

The law of attraction, as made famous in the book and film *The Secret*, is a principle that states that what you think about the most tends to be attracted into your life. Think about good things – money, possessions, good relationships – and you attract those good things. Think about bad things – debt, illness, conflict – and you attract those bad things. Is it true? Is there really some mystical force or universal law of physics that gives you more of what you focus on?

The fact is that some of what's described as the law of attraction definitely operates but you don't need to believe in anything mystical to understand it. There are a number of very practical reasons our thoughts become self-fulfilling prophecies. One of the reasons for this is that, as you may know, the majority of what we communicate to the outside world is actually done so through non-verbal communication (such as body language and tone of voice) rather than words. If you go to a networking meeting in a good state of mind, with a genuine smile on your face and relaxed, open body language, it's likely you'll connect more easily with people than if you turn up miserable, pessimistic, and expecting people to ignore you. And if you spend too much time complaining, you tend to attract other people who complain and turn off others. (This doesn't mean, however, that you should become one of those people that pretend they never have a moment of disappointment or despondency!)

Another reason for the powerful effects of a positive outlook is that your brain is continually filtering the mass of information that comes into your senses according to what your focus is. If you are on the lookout for a way to get into TV presenting, your ears prick up when you overhear someone talking about working in TV, or your eyes are drawn by a newspaper article on a famous TV presenter's career and how they started. If you have convinced yourself, however, that TV is too tough to get into, you're more likely to notice stories about how cutthroat TV is. Whatever your belief is about the world, you tend to notice the supporting evidence for that belief.

So whether or not you choose to believe that the power of quantum physics, the universe, or God is helping you out, there is no doubt that getting clear on what you do want and focusing on that will bring you better results than focusing on what you don't want. The question then is how do you create a more optimistic outlook?

Introducing your nemesis

You cannot successfully survive the roller-coaster to transform your life from worker to player unless you master the inner game of play: those unhelpful doubts, beliefs and habits that hold you back. To do that, you will need to tackle your nemesis.

If you can't work out what you want to do with your life, if others' criticism cuts you to the bone, if you're haunted by negative visions of the future, if you're creatively blocked, if you're a perfectionist or procrastinator, or if your mood takes a dive at the smallest trigger, there's one culprit behind it all.

It's the number one block to playing and it's the enemy of your creativity, happiness and even your wealth. And the enemy is inside of you. It's a sub-personality referred to in Gestalt psychology as the top dog.

The top dog is the part of you that says the most damning things:

'You can't write to save your life.'

'So now you want to be a starving artist?'

'You've always been useless with money.'

'You're mad to change career in a recession.'

'If you quit your job, you'll lose your house and end up living in a cardboard box on the street.'

And if it doesn't come out as words, you might see images in your mind or feel sensations in the body which represent the same message. When you believe and obey these messages, you limit your playfulness, your creativity, your happiness and your life. Every creativity exercise ever invented was designed to get past your top dog.

Others call top dog the internal critic but I find it more helpful to name it as a separate sub-personality. And 'critic' suggests it might give some constructive criticism. The top dog's messages are not constructive.

The top dog grew inside you as a child with repeated messages from your parents and other significant authority figures. The same people who taught you important things like 'Don't run into the road' and 'Keep away from the fire' also taught you less useful ideas like 'All artists are broke', 'You have to sacrifice your happiness to be successful' and 'No one enjoys their job'. Now these messages are a deeply ingrained habit within your own mind; they are the language of your top dog.

The quality of your life is determined by the quality of your internal dialogue.

Pete Cohen, executive coach, trainer and TV presenter

Origins of the top dog

Babies know what they want and express it freely. Hungry? Just scream. They don't have creative blocks. Of course, this isn't a great way for adults to behave so we raise our children to act in a more sociably acceptable way. But sometimes teaching good behaviour isn't done cleanly. It strays into criticism, shame and humiliation: snapping at the boy that cries, laughing at the girl that gets angry, the silent flick of the eyebrows that disapproves of a child 'showing off'. It's these incidences that create your top dog.

In reality these messages were fuelled by the fear and anxiety of the person giving them. And that fear and anxiety was learned in *their* childhood. So your top dog is driven by fear – fear of failing, of 'making a fool of yourself', of getting hurt, of being humiliated.

There's not much logic to it either. It often gives conflicting messages – 'you should stand up for yourself'/'don't make yourself unpopular'. After all, this is a very young part of you. Have you ever seen two young children walking down the street and the elder sibling is admonishing the younger using their parents' language: 'Oh, I don't know what we are going to do with you!' That's all your top dog is doing – aping the messages from your parents.

In a strange way, your top dog is actually trying to protect you – like the person who is self-conscious about their weight and feels compelled to make a joke about it before anyone else does. But the message only serves to make you feel worse.

Top dog messages are culturally influenced. Classic British ones are 'Don't get your hopes up', 'Don't get ideas above your station', 'Don't show off' and even the shockingly unhealthy '"I want" never gets'.

We hypnotise ourselves through these kinds of habitual thoughts into mistaking unhelpful beliefs for facts of life. We become convinced that 'you can only get rich by doing something you don't enjoy' or that you're 'just not one of those lucky people born with talent'. I meet a lot of people with very different beliefs but the one thing they all have in common is that they see their beliefs as the way the world really is. And this is despite the fact that each client believes such different things. Clients tell me 'it's impossible to change career after 30' or '. . . after 40' or '. . . after 50'. And all I can think is 'Well, one of you is wrong!'

Taming your top dog

The greatest mistake we all make is to take the top dog as the voice of reason. It is not. So your first step to managing your top dog for greater creativity and happiness is to identify it. Start today to notice your internal dialogue and if you spot something that might be your top dog, simply label it, 'Ah, that sounds like top dog'.

This is particularly important when you hit a setback. Know your pattern. What are the kinds of things you find most difficult to deal with? When things didn't go your way in the past, what happened? If you gave up, what was the top dog message at the time that discouraged you? If you managed to get back on the horse, what helped you do it? Did you read a motivating book, speak to a friend or just stop thinking about it for a while? Make a note and remember to use it the next time you hit the down cycle. If you have a friend who always cheers you up, put their number on speed dial now!

Sometimes it's not even a setback that's the trigger. Have you ever suddenly lost motivation on something without knowing why? You start off on some project really excited and a little while later feel completely deflated. Or you find you've simply moved on to something else without even thinking about it. Notice what happened to throw you off track; was there something you told yourself without even registering it? This is a top dog message.

The next step is to challenge top dog's messages. When you catch a negative message, think of the more supportive alternative. When top dog says, 'What's the point in starting? You never finish anything', note it and find the counter argument 'Sure I will. I finished a big project last month that looked impossible and I'll finish this one too'. This might sound a little crazy to talk back to yourself, but you're already having an inner dialogue; you might as well make it a more positive one. If you're struggling to find a positive response, imagine you were advising a friend. What would you say to them in this situation?

If you're not sure if a message you've caught is one you should change – perhaps because it appears to be stating the truth – ask yourself, 'Would I say this in exactly this form to a friend?' If not, you shouldn't be saying it to yourself. It's remarkable how we tell ourselves things we would never say to others.

The key is habit. Every time you catch a critical thought and re-member to replace it with a supportive one, you build the habit and make it easier to do it again. Not only that, but you will also affect your own brain chemistry. Every time you have a negative thought, chemicals are released in the brain and the rest of the body that make you feel worse. Every time you have a positive thought, chemicals are released that make you feel good.

This is not something you can change overnight but if you could spend just one whole day interrupting every negative thought and introducing its more supportive opposite, you would find that you were strangely happier that day than at any other recent time – without any special 'reason' to be so. And when you make it a habit, you build structures and connections in the brain that make it easier to do again.

One of the best ways to reinforce your positive internal dialogue is to hang out with supportive people.

Build your support team

Isolation is the dreamkiller.

Barbara Sher, American careers expert and author of five books

What company do you keep? If you want to turn yourself from a worker into a player and escape conventional jobs, you will never do this if the only people you ever spend time with are other people stuck in jobs they don't enjoy. If you're self-employed and struggling to make a living, you will probably never make a good income if all the people you hang out with are struggling too. Why? Because we can't help but take on the opinions, beliefs and habits of the people we spend the most time with. If we're out of step with those around us, what we want will seem abnormal or unusual. Human beings are built to adjust to the people around them. Just remember that you can choose the community you want to fit in with.

When I survey people wanting to do something more creative with their lives, one of their biggest reported challenges is lack of confidence. Whatever it might look like, even the most successful people have to manage their own confidence at times. Here are two important questions I ask clients who are lacking confidence: 'What is your top dog telling you?' and 'Who do you spend time with?' If your top dog often tells you things that shake your confidence, you can counter this by spending time with positive people who will support you in your projects.

You must create your own support team. Find a small group of four or five people to meet with regularly. Use the group to encourage each other, comfort you when you have a setback, and hold you accountable to do what you say you're going to do.

Do you want to know the secret of getting things done when you're totally undisciplined and a chronic procrastinator? Set a release date as we saw in Secret three and ensure that other people hold you to it. Here's how my friend James did it. He wanted to try creating instrumental music for television but knew he was likely to procrastinate on doing it. So he agreed with his creativity group that he would bring a new finished piece of music to their meeting every fortnight and play it to them. If he didn't, he would pay them a forfeit of £50. It's amazing what a little external pressure – even self-created – can accomplish. James met all his deadlines, paid no forfeits and ended up creating more music in that period than at any time before.

Stop imagining you're going to wake up one day with great self-discipline. Instead, start building your own support team now. You can start by just finding one other person who you know will be supportive and will take action. Agree to meet them every two to four weeks. Put the appointment in your diary and agree what each of you will have done by then. Show your results when you meet. You'll be amazed how much work you get done the night before your meeting!

Myth 9: People who are successful don't need support (advice, mentoring, coaching, therapy)

The secret to solo success is . . . it's impossible. You can't achieve anything of any great significance on your own. The myth of the lone entrepreneur who did it all on their own is possibly the most dangerous one yet. The fact is people who want to achieve extraordinary things create extraordinary levels of support for themselves: coaches, trainers, advisers, therapists and inspiring peer groups.

A quick word of warning before we move on: be careful who you share your dreams with. Pick supportive people, not the cynical people critical of everything (cynicism is just a way for very fearful people to manage anxiety). Our instincts are usually pretty good on this if we'll only listen to them.

When someone is damning of your new direction, just reflect for a moment on their lives. How is their career going? What's their life like? Do they enjoy it? Or are they miserable and moaning about it all the time? Even if they enjoy their life, would you want it? If you don't want their results, think twice before taking their advice.

Feeling scared yet?

Decide that you want it more than you are afraid of it.

Bill Cosby

If you're not scared at least some of the time, you're not doing it right. Fear is an inevitable companion when you take the risk to create a different kind of life for yourself. Your ability to manage it is a fundamental factor in how far you can go.

When you start to experience worry, anxiety, or naked terror, this is a great time to call on your support team. Get some calming input from someone reliable and ask for some practical steps you can take.

Check what your top dog is saying that's adding to the fear. Fear is something you *do*, not something that happens. Don't believe me? Think of a jumbo jet full of passengers about to take off. Some of them will feel very afraid, some will feel excited, some will feel bored, some will be asleep. Yet they are all on the same plane. What's the difference? The thoughts and images each individual passenger is creating. The fearful passenger is creating visions of the plane crashing, interpreting each sound as a sign of something wrong and telling themselves that planes crash all the time and that 'I'm not the lucky type'.

Dealing with your fear is one of the most important things you can do. Successful people typically hold an optimistic view of the world and know how to manage what fear they do experience. They also deliberately do the things that still scare them in order to continually slay the demons that hold them back – whether it's giving a public talk, quitting a safe line of work, or even making a radical change of hairstyle.

For 14 years I had this trademark hairstyle where I had a shaved head but long braids in back. And it's funny that after so many years of having the same haircut there was one day at the office when I thought 'You know, I've changed everything else about myself in the last 14 years except this. I wonder why I don't change my haircut. I wonder if I should cut it off . . .' And immediately I had this physical reaction like 'Oh my God! I can't cut it off. This is my trademark. This is what everybody knows me by. If I do that I'll just be ordinary. People will think I've sold out and I'll just look corporate when I'm wearing a suit. I can't cut it off!'

And I was like: 'Damn, listen to me. I am fucking scared aren't I? I am really scared to cut off my braids.' And then immediately I decided, 'Well, therefore I should do it.' And I just went and grabbed some scissors off someone's desk and went into the bathroom and cut them off.

I think it's an important philosophy that whatever scares you, go do it. Because then it won't scare you anymore. And the less things that scare you the better.

Read more of Derek's thoughts on business and life at *sivers.org*

When you're doing OK as you are, it's easy to focus on all the possible risks of doing something new. Just remember when you're afraid of taking a risk that there is a risk to *not* doing something. The risk of not changing your career is that you wake up ten years later and find you're still in a job you dislike. The risk of not taking on an exciting new project is that you are giving up all the wonderful things that would have happened in your life had you dared to do it. You need to be willing to give up the good enough to go for the great.

It is when we all play safe that we create a world of utmost insecurity. It is when we all play safe that fatality will lead us to our doom. It is in the 'dark shade of courage' alone that the spell can be broken.

Dag Hammarskjöld, Secretary General of the United Nations, 1962

How to be indestructible

Chris Guillebeau has created a remarkable life for himself; he travels the world and lives off the blog he writes about his experiences. When I asked him the one behaviour someone most needs if they want to achieve the same kind of success, his answer was just two words, 'Don't stop'.

It's pretty much inevitable you will get what you really want if you just don't stop. Just remember that if you're flexible, there will be more than one way to have the experience you want even if your original vision doesn't pan out.

The key is that with each play project, you keep fine-tuning your trajectory to move closer and closer to getting paid to play. Use the feedback you're getting, both internal and external, to guide you. External feedback includes your results and the critique of others. Internal feedback is what the experience is like for you – is it enjoyable or does it look like it will be when you've got the hang of it? Does it feel like you're in flow?

If you launch a play project and find that you're not enjoying it as much as you hoped, that it doesn't feel like the right direction, or you're not getting the results you expected, don't just quit. Think about how you can change the project to make it work better for you. Something attracted you to this in the first place – don't just throw it out. If you set out to become a public speaker but find that conventional after-dinner speaking isn't working for you, think again what part of the experience originally excited you. How can you get that a different way? If it was the thought of inspiring others, you could try teaching or running small workshops for your next play project. If the experience you wanted was to share your humour, try a stand-up comedy course.

Once you've finished each play project, you'll be in a different place to where you started and your next project can build on this base. By doing this, you can set off without knowing exactly where you're heading and play your way to something that works for you. This is a very different experience from that of people who repeatedly take a few tentative steps in one direction then retreat before shuffling off in a different direction only to return once more to the place where they started.

Life as a player takes plenty of time and effort and it's not going to be 100 per cent fun every day. The whole point is to keep moving on and expanding what you thought you were capable of. This means times of challenge, risk, fear and setbacks.

If you wake up one day and don't feel like doing what you promised someone, you still do it because keeping your promises is an essential part of getting paid to play. If you find you frequently don't feel like doing something, it's time for a change. The good news is that even previously quite boring tasks become more enjoyable when you're doing them for yourself. There's a big difference between having to sweep the floor in some dead-end job and sweeping the floor of the shop you just rented, ready to open it to the public. As Derek Sivers puts it, 'If you're changing somebody else's baby's diapers that feels like work. But if it's your own kid, that doesn't feel like work.'

A fundamental part of the shift from worker to player is to take total responsibility for your own working life. It takes time to stop thinking like a worker and blaming others (or the economy) for your situation. Turn the focus back on yourself and ask again and again 'What can I do to improve this situation?' This is a big shift and can sometimes feel like turning an oil tanker around!

Be willing to have uncomfortable conversations. One of the greatest skills you can learn is to be willing to ask people for what you need. Ask someone to mentor you; ask someone to buy your product or service; ask an employee to redo a piece of work. Sometimes these are not comfortable things to discuss. Most people avoid having uncomfortable conversations; they don't go up to someone famous and ask to talk to them, interview them or work for them. Most people don't cold call a radio station and ask to be interviewed about their project. But then most people don't end up with the life they want. If you do what everyone else does, you'll get what everyone else gets.

Dare to have uncomfortable conversations and you'll soon see how your results differ to others. And if it all goes horribly wrong and you slink away cringing at what just happened, just remember that you dared to do something that most don't. You'll laugh about it later. Probably.

Anyone who has never made a mistake has never tried anything new.

Albert Einstein

Stop asking for permission

Are you stuck in the permission trap? Are you waiting for someone to tell you that what you want is possible? Are you spending a lot of time asking and exploring whether you can do what you want to do? Are you researching options and eliminating them one by one? Are you asking 'Is it possible to have a career in X?', 'Is it crazy to start a business in Y?' 'Could I ever write a book?'

Stop asking *if* you can have what you want, ask '*How* can I have what I want?' When you pose yourself a question, your mind gets to work on answering it even when you're busy doing something else. Ask *whether* you can do something and your mind produces a list of pros and cons. Ask *how* you can do something and your mind comes up with all the ways to do it. Which is going to move you forward? (If after a few days of pondering, the *how* question is still drawing a blank, you can often get unstuck with a *who* question: 'Who would know how to do this?'; 'Who could put me in touch with the right person to move me forward?')

Stop asking for permission from others to do what you want to do, whatever it may be. Decide that you will make it happen and you will do whatever it takes to do so. Then you're thinking like a player.

Take some tips from the world's best expert on your success

When you're facing a challenging project, consult the best expert in the world on your success – you. Look back at how you achieved all your life's significant achievements to date: finding your home, making the move, finding your partner, making your relationship work, how you've got a new job or got over a difficult illness. What did you do that made these achievements possible? What worked? How can you use the same strategies now?

When I look back, I realise that pretty much everything I have ever achieved has been due to two factors. Firstly, I started on the project simply because I was interested in it, and then I finished it because I had an external deadline to share the results that could not be moved. The deadline was the only way to get over my natural perfectionism and procrastination. I made the final decision on my first home and bought it in the two weeks before I quit my job so that I could honestly say I was employed when I signed the mortgage. If I didn't it might have been very difficult to get a mortgage at all. For every achievement, there was usually a gun to my head, figuratively speaking. I'd love to say this wasn't so but knowing that it is, I can use it to my advantage. Now I know to always agree a release date with other people: a date that I simply have to meet.

Tim Smit, creator of the Eden Project, has achieved an enormous amount and yet describes himself as 'fundamentally lazy' and 'one of the least focused people you could ever meet'. I asked him what drives him to take on these projects rather than just taking it easy. His answer? 'The fear of death and a rash desire to make unlikely promises. Which I then have to fulfil or lose face as a consequence.'

What works for you? It might be making it fun, or getting loads of support, or getting expert advice. Whatever it is, use it now.

How to cheat

If you want to accelerate your journey to getting paid to play, try cheating. If someone else has ever successfully done what you're trying to do, chances are you can too. How did they do it? Steal their strategies. Don't steal the content of what they did, steal *how* they did it. How did that relatively new band get known so quickly? How did that person get into advertising with so little prior experience? How did that software start-up get going without venture capital? Find out, then copy it.

Myth 10: Famous people are just different from me

Of course none of this will help you if you're in the habit of thinking of the very famous and successful as a different species. They're human just like you. Sure, talent is a factor but often a lot less than you think. Model their beliefs, thoughts, behaviours and language and you'll be on the way to modelling their success. Be wary of assuming that successful people had some advantage (money, connections, status) that you don't. There will be someone somewhere who had no more advantage than you and still made it. Find them and model them.

Take the Millionaire Test to stay on track

As you play out your journey to doing what you really want to do for a living, check in every day on how it's going and adjust your course accordingly. How do you do this? By using the Millionaire Test.

At the beginning of the day when you first wake up, ask yourself these two questions:

1. If I was already a millionaire, would I choose to do what I am about to do today?

Write down your response.

2. If I had a blank diary today and all the money I could want, what would I *choose* to do with this day?

Write down your response.

If the response is that you would actually the take day off and sit on a beach, then ask how you can achieve some of that experience. Can you actually take the day off? If not, can you find some space to do nothing? If you're nowhere near a beach, can you go swimming after work and then sit by the pool reading a book? Or should you make time to book your next holiday today?

If the Millionaire Test keeps showing that you wouldn't choose to do your work today, it's time to change your work.

You can also use the Millionaire Test throughout the day for the smaller decisions you make. I went to a networking event recently with lots of 'important' people from big companies. I found myself thinking, 'I should go speak to that guy from the multinational corporation, he could be an important contact'. The problem was I ended up having conversations I wasn't really interested in; I realised I was bored. I was choosing people I thought I *should* talk to, not the ones I really wanted to – a habit ingrained from my years of consultancy work in big corporations.

Then I remembered my mantra,

> If I were already a millionaire, would I do this thing I am
> considering right now?

I realised that if I was already a millionaire I would just talk to
whoever looked interesting to me or who I knew was involved in a
project I genuinely wanted to know about. I started to do this that
night and met a couple of great people and had fascinating conversations – ones that spurred new ideas and new connections for
my business, connections I would *love* to make. One of the people I
spoke to went on to speak at my Scanners Night event.

Imagine what would happen if we always worked on this basis.
We would make natural connections with people we enjoy spending time with. Our projects or businesses would continue to grow
with less strain and a lot more fun.

Moment by moment, this simple, rather materialistic-sounding
question will guide you towards getting paid to play. On the way
it's still important, obviously, to do the things you promised even
when you're not in the mood for it. And you might take some projects that are not exactly what you would choose to do but are a
good stepping stone to get you to your ultimate ideal.

Of course, you could just ask the question 'Do I really feel like doing
this?' but it's amazing how many of my clients cannot answer questions like that effectively – thanks to the influence of the top dog.

If you want to make a habit of using the Millionaire Test, carry
around a reminder of it. You may need to change the wording to
work for you. 'Millionaire' can mean many things but to my mind
implies a level of established wealth that, while not allowing you
to retire for good, would give you a great quality of living without
working for several years. This is a good position from which to
make choices about your work – the heat is off but you may still
need to work further down the line.

How to make progress when you've got no time and no energy

Are you struggling to find the time for your project? Are you creating a new career while still busy working in your old one? There is a way you can still keep making progress: by doing little and often. Carve out micro-blocks of super-focused time to do what is most important to move you forward. Could you spare ten minutes of time at some point in the next 24 hours? You'll be surprised at what you can do in just ten minutes when you're prepared and you focus completely on the task in hand. If you come home exhausted at the end of a day at your current work, you might not feel like doing anything. The fact is that motivation often comes *after* you start something, not before.

Here's how to keep going even when you have very little time to invest. This also works brilliantly if you have a task you've been putting off because you have some kind of resistance to it.

1. Think of the next task you need to do to move your play project forward. What single thing will have the biggest impact for the least amount of time spent? Write it down.

2. Decide how long your micro-block will be: 10 minutes? 20? 30?

3. Write down what you can do in this micro-block. Don't go writing things like 'Learn French' or 'Plan business'. Write 'Do exercise 10 in French book', 'Search online for three good articles on making money from a blog and print them to read later', 'Read the three articles printed yesterday'.

4. Get out your diary and write it in as a real appointment: e.g. 7:00 to 7:15 Do French Exercise 10.

5. Turn up for your appointment. Make this as real a commitment as if you had a doctor's appointment. If something absolutely critical comes up you might move it, but otherwise you stick to it. You never just skip it.

6. Switch off your phone, your email and anything else you don't need that might distract you. Tell others who might interrupt that you are busy.

7. Use this brilliant tip from time management guru Mark Forster: get a kitchen timer that counts down and set it to ten minutes or whatever time you've allocated. Place the timer right in front of you and set it counting down. This will help keep you focused.

8. Do exactly what you wrote down that you were going to do.

9. When the timer goes off, you can stop – even if you haven't finished the task. (But if you're now feeling motivated to continue, do.)

10. Before you file your notes, or close your document, decide what you will do in your next micro-block. Write it down as your next action so that when you pick-up again tomorrow, you know exactly what you're doing. Put your project away some place where you can pick it up again quickly.

11. Get out your diary and write in the appointment for your next micro-block and the action you will take in it.

12. Go and relax!

Of course, for any significant project you're likely to need some big blocks of time to get it done, but until you can free up that time, you will be amazed how much progress you make in your micro-blocks. And the continual progression will keep your spirits up much more than watching days disappear without doing anything. How many weeks go by with you waiting to spend an hour on your project but never finding the time? Now, can you imagine doing ten minutes a day, six days a week? Author Suzy Greaves managed to write her entire book *The Big Peace* in 15-minute segments between running her successful life-coaching business and being a mum.

You don't need to know exactly how you're going to achieve your project. You only need to know the next action and then turn up and do it. Your success is pretty much guaranteed if you do. Just keep moving forward and adjust your course according to your results.

Try doing a micro-block first thing in the morning before you start anything else. It's a great way to start your day and ensures nothing can get in the way of doing it. If you can grow the block of time to an hour every day, you can make a huge amount of progress on your project. Be sure to use this technique on Play Wednesday too.

Manage your overwhelm, not your time

It's easy to get overwhelmed these days. We have all too much to do and too much information to manage. Even with the discipline to be ruthless with your tasks and information, the problem will never go away. Your to-do list will not all be ticked off when you die!

Overwhelm is one of your greatest obstacles on the way to getting paid to play. And creative people are particularly prone to it. Why? Because the creative personality does not think in a structured way. We don't have a strong sense of time. We get absorbed in something and hours fly by. It's the ability to forget time altogether that allows us to go so deeply into the creative process. We don't naturally think in a sequential way. We can see everything needed to make a project happen but without any time-frame, so everything looks like it needs to be done right away. The result is overwhelm. Overwhelm feels terrible, so when it happens our response is often to stop altogether; we collapse in a heap or more subtly, we find we've started browsing YouTube or watching TV – anything to take our mind off the overwhelm. This is why overwhelm often passes for procrastination or, worse, laziness.

I think of this as an inbuilt tilt switch. To be a great pinball player, you have to shake the machine around a bit. But if you hit it too hard, the tilt switch activates and the whole machine shuts down. Your job is to notice when your tilt switch has activated, realise it's overwhelm, and do something to address it. The answer is always to break down your task into smaller chunks and focus only on the next chunk you have to do.

Have you found yourself watching TV when you've promised yourself you'd plan your whole website today? Break it down. What's the first thing you have to do? Make it something that lasts no more an hour. How about choosing what five pages you're going to create? Or writing the three main points you want to make on the homepage.

If you get stuck, call in someone who finds it easy to plan their time. They'll quickly be able to look at what you have on your plate and tell you the first five things to do and in what order.

Moment by moment you can do simple things to reduce your overwhelm. Have a good diary. Write everything down; don't carry essential information in your head. Leave it free for thinking. Be realistic; write short lists for each day with the three things that are most important to do.

Also check what your top dog is saying about this task that has overwhelmed you. Is it something pessimistic? If it's telling you the project is bound to fail, or you should have done this ages ago, you won't be very motivated to work on it. Is it about perfectionism? Perfectionists are even more prone to overwhelm because their top dog tells them everything they do must be flawless. It's better to finish something that's good than to abandon yet another project because you can't make it perfect.

How to manage your brilliant ideas

Do you have more ideas than you know what to do with? If you pursue everything you think of, you'll never get anything finished.

Create a place to keep all your good ideas. When a new one comes to you, store it where you know you'll be able to find it so you can get on with what you were doing.

When you start a whole new project, the very first thing you should do is create a repository for all the ideas you'll have: whether it's a talk you've just been booked to do, a website you're going to build or product you've decided to make. Start a fresh notebook, or do as I do and start a blank text file on your computer. Then whenever you have another idea, open the file and jot it down. You might find the first draft of your talk almost writes itself.

When you have a great idea and you know you want to press 'Go' on it, don't hang around.

> *What you actually do within 24 hours of having a creative idea will spell the difference between success and failure.*
>
> **Buckminster Fuller**

Ideas have a half-life. Wait too long before you act on them and there's a chance you'll look back at your notes and wonder what on earth you were talking about. If it looks like the right project for you now to get paid to play, don't waste time getting it launched. 'Money likes speed', as author Joe Vitale likes to say.

How to be a creative genius

All children are artists. The problem is how to remain an artist once we grow up.

Pablo Picasso

Learn the tricks to unlock your own creative genius and you'll produce far grander results for a lot less effort. Don't believe the myths about creativity. It's easy to assume great works of art fell out of their creator complete, but in fact they are far more often *sculpted*. Sculptures start as a shapeless block of marble. The sculptor chips away week by week until a rough form starts to emerge. Eventually, the final form is revealed in all its beauty. Any creative process works in a similar, iterative way but it's easy to forget this and expect we can create something brilliant in one sitting. Here's a much better way.

1. **Get clear what problem you are trying to solve** or what outcome you want to achieve. 'A problem well defined is half solved', as psychologist John Dewey once said.

2. **Work on your project a little every day**, ideally first thing in the morning. In between, your subconscious will work on it. Aid it by doing something simple and physical – walking, gardening, washing up.

3. **Record your ideas**. Creativity researcher Dr Robert Epstein says that those we consider creative may simply have good 'capturing skills': that is, they take all their ideas seriously and record them. So take your playbook and pen everywhere and note anything that comes to you about your project whether it's in bed, on the train or at work. You can even buy a waterproof notepad to capture those great ideas you have in the shower!

4. **Think *quantity* not *quality***. 'The best way to have a good idea is to have lots of ideas', as chemist and peace activist Linus Pauling once said (and he's one of the few people in the world to have won two Nobel Prizes). Generate as many ideas as possible, write for a set period of time per day, or take a set number of photos per week. This takes the pressure off you getting it 'right' and thereby generates more creative results. Later, go back and choose your best results. Always keep the processes of creating and editing separate as they require different modes of thinking. One is adding to your content, the other is taking it away. Try to do both at the same time and you end up with a brain-freeze.

5. **If you get stuck, brainstorm with friends or colleagues** and remember that no idea is too wacky in a brainstorm. Or try talking about it to someone for ten minutes while they simply listen. If on your own, try writing continuously on the topic without stopping for ten minutes and see what comes out.

When I tried my hand at stand-up comedy, people would ask me how I came up with my material. And I would tell them it's not as difficult as you might think. Carry around a notebook and write everything you can think of that might be funny whenever it occurs to you. Then try the material out on people and edit out the weak stuff. You'll eventually be left with five minutes of good material you can go and perform.

The power of 'creative idling'

Idleness for me is not a giving up on life but a spirited grabbing hold of it.

Tom Hodgkinson, editor of The *Idler* and author of *How to be idle*

Idle time is an essential part of the creative process. There will be times you need to put a huge amount of effort into a project. Taking breaks, doing something completely different, spending some time playing with your children, and bunking off for the afternoon can all help you refresh. It's also just a kinder way to treat yourself. If you're going to be your own boss you might as well be a nice one!

Remember to build some time into your schedule for some pure play – the things you love without worrying about turning it into an income. Notice your natural pace and work with it, not against it. Don't try to make yourself into someone else: someone who can work all night, or can focus for four hours straight, or works normal office hours. Work *with* who you are. If you want better results, your job is to *do* something different, not *be* someone different.

Listen to your body when it's asking for a break. If you don't, you'll find yourself stealing the rest time anyway by losing your attention or getting distracted by something unimportant. You can't cheat your body for very long so you might as well take a real break. You might even get your big breakthrough when you do. J.K. Rowling was travelling alone on a delayed train from Manchester to London when 'the idea for Harry Potter simply fell into my head'. Over the next four hours 'all the details bubbled up in my brain, and this scrawny, black-haired, bespectacled boy who didn't know he was a wizard became more and more real to me'.

Physicist Richard Feynman was watching someone messing around throwing a plate in the air in Cornell University's cafeteria when he decided to describe its wobbling movement in equations 'for fun'. The spinning plate equations turned out to be critical to his study of quantum electrodynamics, the work that went on to win the Nobel Prize.

> *It's necessary to be slightly underemployed if you are to do something significant.*
>
> **James D. Watson, co-discoverer of the structure of DNA**

Get a little closer to your natural way of working every day. How close can you get to the way you envisioned living in your year out?

Go on, take a nap

You must sleep sometime between lunch and dinner . . . That's what I always do. Don't think you will be doing less work because you sleep during the day. That's a foolish notion held by people who have no imaginations. You will be able to accomplish more.

Winston Churchill

If you're going to be idle, why not go all the way and take a nap? Naps have been shown in research trials to lower stress hormones and boost productivity and creativity. The effect of a nap is like rebooting your brain and, as Winston Churchill said, 'You get two days in one – well, at least one and a half'.

If anyone tries to make you feel guilty about napping in the middle of a workday, just remind them that sleep can also be a very productive time. Paul McCartney dreamed the melody for 'Yesterday', and chemist Friedrich August Kekulé discovered the baffling ring shape of the chemical compound benzene after dreaming about a snake biting its own tail. Good napping takes practice. I can now get to sleep in five minutes or less. Use a timer to keep the nap short, around 20 minutes, and you won't wake up groggy.

When you've got the hang of all this, you're in a good place to start angling your play towards something you can get paid for. Read the next chapter to find out how.

Put it into play

Keys to this secret:

→ Dare to hope you can get what you really want and deal with the setbacks when they happen. You guarantee your success if you just don't stop.

→ Identify your top dog and start to tame it.

→ Create your support team and manage your fear.

→ Model other people's successful strategies and your own.

→ Use the Millionaire Test to stay on track.

→ Do little and often if you're short of time and manage your overwhelm.

→ Use the creative genius process and creative idling to maximise your effectiveness.

What you should have now:

➡ a strategy to manage yourself to get you where you want to go.

Take ten minutes to play:

➡ Try putting one of the strategies in this chapter into action now.

➡ Call one person who could be the start of your support team.

Exclusive extras on ScrewWorkLetsPlay.com

➡ more on your top dog;

➡ interviews with creative entrepreneurs;

➡ the secret of good napping;

➡ where to buy a waterproof notepad and a good countdown timer.

Secret five
How to play for profit . . . and purpose

An entrepreneur is someone who solves problems at a profit.

T. Harv Eker, American entrepreneur, author and speaker

We've now seen how to launch your first play project and manage yourself to keep going when things get tricky. This chapter will show you how to tune your projects towards something people might actually pay you for. To kick us off, here's a story of a British entrepreneur who created an innovative business around a challenge he'd experienced in his own life.

From an idea on a beach to a national business

Richard Alderson is founder of Careershifters, a ground-breaking British business supporting people making a major career change. But how did he get the idea and how did he know it would work as a business?

> *It was the tail end of 2003 and I'd just been through the painful but ultimately rewarding process of leaving the corporate job I was in at the time. I was in Kerala taking a career break and ful-filling one of my dreams of studying yoga for a couple of months. Twisting my body into new shapes also had the interesting ef-fect of making some exciting ideas pop out of my head.*
>
> *In early 2004 I wrote an initial business plan (quite an unsophis-ticated one as I was later to realise) and started to pitch the idea to a select group of friends and colleagues around me, refining it as I went. I then started to approach and get initial support*

from some of the people that had inspired me in my change – authors of some of the books I'd read, coaches who'd helped me, and others who I considered to be leading people in the career change field.

Later that year, I began pulling a team of people around me who I thought might be able to help me make the project a reality. Most of them were career changers themselves, all of them shared my passion for making this happen, and they all, like me, volunteered their time to the project over and above their day jobs.

We had our first team meeting in a bar in Soho on a cold night in February 2005 and have been meeting monthly since, sometimes in spare office meeting rooms, sometimes in bars, sometimes in my flat.

It hasn't all been easy. There were times where things were moving at a snail's pace when I wondered what on earth I was doing pumping so many hours of my life into the enterprise. But, stubborn person that I am, I never wanted to give up because I truly believed that we were creating something that could help thousands of people.

I believe Careershifters fills a much-needed gap in the market. There's currently no other dedicated online community for career changers. There's nowhere else online where you can access practical advice from so many experts in the field, where you can connect with so many other career shifters and where you can get inspired by so many different stories of people who've made successful changes. We're also one of a new breed of more-than-profit companies, whose purpose is to create social impact alongside a sustainable business.

And here we are now, almost six years after I came up with the idea – we've got a fantastic website, the brand new Careershifters Guide, workshops running in London (soon to be spreading across the UK) and the Careershifters Club about to launch.

2010 is set to be our year of growth and our mission is to help 1000 change career in 2010. I thought it would take half the time to get to this stage, but that's what they always say, right?

Find out more about Careershifters at *careershifters.org*

Richard had an idea that he thought could both make a sustainable business and help a lot of people with something he had experienced himself. So how can you do this? How can you find a way to turn the things you really enjoy doing into something people will pay for? This is where we get into the nitty-gritty of making money. It's time to start thinking like an entrepreneur. Are you ready to discover the magic key to getting paid for playing? Here it is:

Solve a problem.

If you want to turn your playing into profit, the key is to do the things you love doing in ways that solve problems for people. Problems are powerful things. Find a good problem to solve and you can bet there'll be a way to make money out of it. Solving people's problems happens to feel good too.

Understanding the power of problems will have a transformational effect on your ability to get paid to play. Here's why. Think about why people spend money. It's predominantly for one of only two reasons: we either want to avoid some pain or experience some pleasure. And out of the two, pain is the far more powerful driver. The pain could be physical (like back pain), emotional (loneliness, unhappiness, boredom), financial (can't afford the next mortgage payment) or even spiritual (feeling unfulfilled). Whether the pain is mild like feeling bored or something more acute like a toothache, it points to a problem that someone is motivated to pay to solve. Think of home insurance – we buy it not because it feels great to be insured but because we feel anxious not to be. Worrying about losing all your belongings if you got burgled is a problem; and it's one that most of us are willing to spend money to solve.

In fact, you could argue that all purchases are made to alleviate some discomfort, even luxury ones. How many holidays are booked in the depths of January when the country is at its darkest and coldest?

People creating their own income for the first time often miss the importance of solving problems. They make the mistake of offering services that are a 'nice to have' not a 'must-have'. If you do this, you'll find it very difficult to make a living. We've all seen the inventor peddling some contraption that's terribly clever but that no one really needs, or the new freelancer offering some service that sounds very nice but no one ever buys. The problem is that something will always be more important than buying what you're offering. People today are busy; we all have long 'to do' lists and overflowing email inboxes. That can be either good news or bad news for you. Make sure you offer something that's already on people's to-do lists and it's good news.

Richard recognised with Careershifters that 'too many people were stuck in jobs that were making them miserable. Fear, finances, lack of confidence, not knowing what their options were and not knowing who or what to turn to for guidance were all holding them back.' This was a real problem for a lot of people: one that featured prominently on their list of concerns to do something about.

When somebody knows they have a problem, you don't have to convince them they need a solution – they already want one. You only need to show them that you are capable of providing that solution and that it's worth the price you're asking. Don't waste your time offering things you have to persuade people they need in the first place. It can be done, but it's very hard work and you may end up broke before you succeed!

Let's go problem hunting

Look at the project you've chosen to play with. Hopefully you've based it on something you think you will enjoy doing and you also have some talent for. The question now is what problem could this project solve for people? Here are some examples of how to identify the problem you solve while doing what you love.

Enjoy building attractive little websites? You could solve the common problem of people feeling overwhelmed by all the options and expenses of building a website by offering website design with a set number of simple customisable designs.

Love writing and blogging? What's the overarching problem you're interested in exploring in the blog? People wanting to dress fashionably but having no money for designer labels? Connecting people who are passionate about a social cause that's currently poorly understood? People wanting to use new services like Twitter but don't know how to start and are worried about getting it wrong?

Enjoy sorting out other people's messy lives? Thinking of becoming a virtual assistant? What problem would you find interesting to help with? People overwhelmed by the complexity of organising events? People who are driven to distraction by their admin tasks interrupting their creative projects?

Passionate about practising complementary therapies? You could specialise in a specific problem area such as helping pregnant women who commonly suffer fatigue, stress and back pain.

Love creating art? Think art doesn't solve a problem? Artist Jay Versluis created a gorgeous abstract photograph called 'Stripes'. An interior designer saw his photo and realised it solved a problem for a new minimalist office development she was working on. The office was crying out for a striking piece of art to offset the stark simplicity of the building. Jay created a backlit installation of the piece measuring a huge 12 feet by 12 feet and ended up making over £5,000.

Invented a quirky gadget that might make a good corporate gift? Lots of companies, both big and small, fear being seen as unimaginative or old-fashioned. This problem means they have to keep finding ways to be different and original in everything they do – including the corporate gifts they give away at exhibitions and events. The problem of being seen as just the same as everyone else should not be underestimated – and of course it's one that individuals have too.

Having fun creating a website of humorous writing, images, or video? Even this can solve a real problem – the problem of being bored at work, wanting to escape for a few moments and have a laugh. If the humour is narrowly focused on an obscure hobby or interest, it can also address the isolation people might otherwise feel and provide a sense of community. (For a nice example, take a look at xkcd.com, a webcomic about mathematics and life.)

Think about your current play project. What problem could this solve for people? When you're looking for a problem to solve, look for the emotional language used by the people you're trying to help. They use words like 'I'm sick of . . .', 'I'm bored with . . .', 'I'm worried about . . .'. When you hear this language, you've found a problem.

Finding the problem

When Sophie Boss launched her business Beyond Chocolate to help women stop yo-yo dieting, the strap line was 'Transform Your Relationship With Food'. She later attended a marketing workshop and as Sophie says,

> *The woman leading it looked at me and said 'You know, I don't think anybody wakes up in the morning thinking "I really must transform my relationship with food!"' And she was right. What they do is they think 'I've got to lose weight' or 'I've just got to stop this dieting madness' or 'I can't do this anymore'. And so we decided to change our wording.*

The strap line of the book we wrote afterwards is 'Stop yoyo dieting and lose weight for good'. It felt like we were making a big compromise because even though women do lose weight with Beyond Chocolate, we didn't feel that was the focus of our work. We were keen to explain how Beyond Chocolate was different and how it could help them. What I've discovered is that people are interested in what they want, and they don't necessarily want to know how we do it. Transforming their relationship with food is the 'how', their goal was to end the misery of yo-yo dieting and finally lose weight.

If you're already self-employed, you might have been offering your services for some time but still be dissatisfied with the take-up. Thinking in the terms of the people you're helping, as Sophie did, could well transform your ability to draw people in and win work. Here's a very powerful way for you to identify the problem you solve. Think about the moment that someone finally buys your product or calls you up and hires you. What is happening to them at that exact moment? They may have been thinking about buying your product or booking some of your time for a while but something precipitates them to finally take the plunge. Do you know what it is? I get the most enquiries about careers consultations on a Monday when people go back to work after the weekend and are faced with just how unhappy they are in their job. (Those that really hate their work contact me Sunday night when just the thought of going back to work is too much!) And I've put this knowledge to good use; I get a good response when I email people on a Monday with a headline that asks, 'Can't face another week at work?'

Now let's find the problem that you can solve for people. We're looking for that sweet spot where the things you love doing, and have some natural talent for, can be used to help people with something that's bugging them. It's time for some serious brainstorming.

Write a big list of problems you reckon you could help with. You don't need to have the complete solution to a problem, but just be able to make some impact on it.

Ask yourself these questions to get you thinking and write down your answers in your playbook.

➡ Look at the play project you defined in Secret three and ask yourself what problem this could solve for other people. What problem could you solve if you changed the focus a little?

➡ Is there a specific industry, niche or group of people you think you'd enjoy working with? If so, what kind of problems do they talk about having? What's the biggest headache in that field right now?

➡ Look back at your moments of magic. What problem (big or small) were you helping people with at that moment?

➡ Within your own life, what problems consistently irritate you that you are well positioned to help with and you might enjoy working on?

➡ If you've already got an idea for a business, write down the most important problems this business could solve for your clients or customers.

➡ If you're already self-employed, what pressing problems do your clients have that you know you could help with? Think of the services or products you already offer and write down the problems that they solve for your clients.

➡ If you currently consult to other businesses (or would like to), what are the pressing problems they have that you can help with? What is going on at the moment people pick up the phone to hire you? You can bet it's a pressing problem! (When I was an independent consultant, finally realising the problem I solved for clients made it much easier to know exactly where to look for work.)

➡ If you're selling yourself in to large organisations, what problem does the person have who is hiring you? You may want to run a workshop to improve staff morale but you must discover what problem their manager sees: perhaps a decrease in performance.

➡ Think of your favourite projects that you have done before. What problem did they solve?

➡ If your aim is to create a better job for yourself (more on this later), what problem is big enough inside the organisation that people would be willing to hire you to work on?

➡ And always check: is this a problem someone has right now? Are they aware of it? Does it feature on their to-do list?

➡ Start to notice successful businesses you admire and ask yourself what problems they solve. You might not see that they are solving a problem at first but think it through; what problems, for example, does Facebook address that makes 300 million people around the world want to use it?

The mistake many people make when first introduced to this way of thinking is that they describe what the person wants, not what their current problem is. If you enjoy helping people make more money, 'wanting to be rich' is not the problem, nor is 'not being rich'. The problem is something more like 'being fed up with working long hours just to make ends meet and still having to go without a decent holiday'. What we're looking for is the pain or discomfort that people are experiencing *right now*.

Some people think talking about problems like this is being too negative or even manipulative. In fact it is more empathic – it is speaking the language of your customers or followers instead of talking from your perspective all the time. If, for example, I constantly feel under the weather, you will have much more impact on me if you talk about the experience of being fed up with a never-ending series of colds and viruses than if you talk to me about how wonderful it is to be in perfect health. It's difficult for me relate to the ideal end result right now. Once you have my attention, of course, then you can start to convince me how you could help me have much better health.

If you struggle to think in terms of the negative state your customers are in, and naturally think in positive terms of what they want, try asking yourself these two questions: what is the thing your customers really want in their lives that you can help them get? Now what is it that's currently stopping them from getting it? It's this obstacle that is the real problem you're solving. For example if you're a personal trainer, your clients want to be fit, healthy and look good. The obstacle (and therefore the problem you solve) is the fact that they don't have the self-discipline or the expertise to easily get fit on their own. Whatever your work is, write down your clients' desire and the obstacle that stops them achieving it without you. You'll find you have far better results when you talk with prospective clients not just about their desires but about this obstacle that stops them getting it.

Knowing the pressing problems of your target market is a hugely valuable thing. If you don't know what they are, run some informal market research. This is surprisingly simple and effective. If you're selling to individuals, send all your contacts an email asking the question 'What's your single biggest challenge right now with clutter / losing weight / winning more business [or whatever your area of interest is]?' The resulting information is priceless. You now know exactly what troubles the people you want to work with most and can set about creating something to help.

If you're selling to organisations, it may be better to arrange to meet a few of them on the understanding that you are doing research and ask them 'What is the biggest single challenge you face in your industry right now?' Again, not only do you get some fantastically useful information but also this non-salesy approach often has a very nice side-effect that someone might say 'Oh, can you actually help us with this now?'

Want to change the world?

Are you fed up with doing work you don't really care about? Are you looking for something more meaningful? Perhaps you already know there is some part of the world you want to have a positive impact on? If so, make it manageable by choosing a specific problem to solve first. This might be a practical problem: restaurants being unfriendly to children; the high-profile failure of public construction projects to come in on time and on budget; technology being far too complicated to use for elderly users; the shocking diet of school children at school and at home.

It might be a global problem: the contribution of inefficient home heating to global warming; the lack of HIV and Aids education in some of the poorest parts of the world; the lack of understanding between different faiths.

Or you might be drawn to helping people with one of the universal challenges of the human condition: loss, illness, relationship problems, low self-esteem, depression. Often the thing we feel most strongly about is something we have experienced ourselves in some form: think of Richard Alderson using his difficult experience of career change to create Careershifters.

Sometimes those challenges that marked our earliest lives leave the biggest impact. Some of us endured poverty, or survived illness, suffered an early loss, or were criticised or discouraged by those most important to us. What challenges have you struggled with in your life? The problem you choose to work on might be informed by this experience.

Which problem to solve?

Hopefully you've identified a number of problems you could help solve for people. How do you choose? Here are five questions to help you decide.

1. **Can I address this problem while doing something that I really enjoy and I'm good at?** If you're just starting out on the journey to get paid to play, this question is the most important one right now. Choose something fun to do.

2. **Do I have something I bring that can impact this problem?** What talents, skills and knowledge do I already have that will be valuable?

3. **Is this a big enough problem for people?** Generally speaking, the bigger the problem and the bigger the impact you can have on it, the more you can get paid for helping with it. Is it the kind of problem people will pay to solve? (If not, it may still be possible to make it work by attracting enough people and charging for advertising or selling other services.)

4. **Are there plenty of people who have this problem right now?** Do I know the kind of people who have this problem? Are they reachable? This is particularly important if you want to solve a relatively mild problem like boredom; you might need to solve it for a lot of people to make it pay.

5. **Is it something I care about addressing?** If you feel strongly about helping people who have this problem, that's all the better. Is there a problem on your list that you look at and think 'I really want to do something about this', then that's a yes – as long as the other criteria are also met.

Make some notes in your playbook about the problems you will help solve but remember that it's likely to take some time and some investigation to really nail this. Keep coming back to this and clarifying over it over the next few weeks and months.

Once you know what you're going to do for people, all you need to do is find 'em and tell 'em. The next chapter will help do you this by showing you how to play the fame game.

Put it into play

Keys to this secret:

➡ The secret to playing for profit is to solve a problem.

➡ If you don't know what problem to solve, ask the people you work with (or intend to work with) what their biggest problems are.

➡ If you want to change the world, choose a specific problem to address.

What you should have now:

➡ a shortlist of problems you can solve and a favourite one to start with or to investigate further.

Take ten minutes to play:

➡ Think of someone who has the problem you want to help solve. Call them up and arrange to talk to them about it; find out exactly what the problem is and what kind of solution they would like. Don't try to sell them anything!

➡ Try writing out a description of the problem which you could later use in an article or blog post for publicity.

Exclusive extras on ScrewWorkLetsPlay.com

➡ Listen to an audio recording that goes deeper into the topic of identifying problems to solve.

➡ Listen to a talk by Sophie Boss about the creation and development of her business Beyond Chocolate.

➡ Read more about Richard Alderson's business Careershifters.

Secret six
How to play the fame game – and win

I am successful because I was willing to give up being anonymous.

Sophia Loren, actress

You should now have some idea of how you can do something that feels like play to you while also providing something people need. All you have to do now is get the message out to those people. And to do that you need to become famous, or at least known, for something. Whether you long to become a household name or simply be respected in your field, you can play the game your way to create the fame you want. This chapter will show you what to say, who to say it to, and where, when and how to say it.

And you'll be amazed at just what you can become famous for today.

icanhascheezburger.com – famous for lolcats

icanhascheezburger.com is a hugely popular website featuring pictures of cats with funny captions (otherwise known as lolcats). Here is a message about the business from the owners as recently posted on their own site.

> *In September of 2007, we launched our company with this amazing community. And at the onset of the worst economic crisis of our time, I quit my day job in order to run ICHC from my living room couch. Cheezburger Network is now one of the largest blog networks in the world. Our second book, How to Take Over Teh Wurld is still on the New York Times bestseller list for the 4th week in a row. Thanks to you, our users, we've grown to more than 20 sites and now reach more than 11 million people around the globe every month.*

Today also marks another milestone for us. When we began, we didn't know what we wanted to be when we grew up. We didn't even know who we were. We're far from grown up, but we know more about who we are and why we're here. We want to enable you to share your sense of humor, share what you find funny with each other and the rest of the world. We want to make you happy for a few minutes each day. This is now the mission of the Cheezburger Network . . .

From the bottom of the hearts of the 26 bloggers, moderators, developers and staff of the Cheezburger Network, thank you.

Ben Huh
CEO
Cheezburger Network

I wonder if Ben and his friends ever told their careers adviser that they wanted to make a living out of funny cat pictures – and what the response would have been if so.

Whatever your vision of fame, your journey to get there is likely to take a while but you can launch it today. The rules have changed; you no longer have to create the perfect finished product before you start to share your work with the world. The internet has changed everything. Now you can play out your ideas in public on a global stage. You can open up the process and share the output of your project as you work on it. You can invite anyone in the world to contribute to it. Play it out as a work in progress, build a tribe of followers, get valuable input, and explore ways to make money from it.

Life in perpetual beta

To be a player is to embrace 'life in perpetual beta', as life coach turned filmmaker Melissa Pierce calls it. She is creating a documentary about how technology enables us to live less planned and more passionate lives. And she's living her message by figuring out what she's doing along the way. At the start she had no real experience of filmmaking; in her first interview, with author Daniel Pink, Melissa unwittingly shakes the camera up and down when she nods in agreement with her interviewee. She started without a definite plan of where she was heading and despite this it's already looking good. She's interviewed the current thought leaders in technology, business, and entrepreneurial culture and released much of the content for free online as the film progresses.

The whole film was sourced through Twitter and other social media, from donations to fund it, to discussions on what to ask the next interviewee. Melissa is now in editing and has already been invited to speak at the prestigious SXSW Interactive conference in Texas.

Find out more about Melissa's project at *lifeinperpetualbeta.com*

Even big companies like Google release everything as 'beta' and implement improvements on the fly. Leading trend firm, Trendwatching, calls this *foreverism:* consumers and businesses embracing conversations, lifestyles and products that are never 'done'.

This is good news for you because when you're just starting out you don't know what your project or business really is yet. Play it out, explore, experiment. Find your unique voice, discover your brand. Invite feedback as blog comments and tweets. As soon as your idea is exposed to the air, it will change; it must change as you discover what others see as the real value in your idea.

Got an idea for a billion-dollar brand? Start with a blog. Talk about the brand's values and who's out there that fits and who doesn't. Want to run an event? List your first as a freebie on meetup.com or as a Facebook event. Want to share your expertise? Sign up at Twitter and start sharing it in bite-size portions every day. Offer to answer people's questions and compile your answers for publication as a book or information product later.

What was once a one-sided conversation from business to customer or star to fan is now a two-way discussion. Musician Moby is allowing people to preview his new album online and even download the title track for free in exchange for posting a review to Twitter in 140 characters. Up-and-coming English singer-songwriter Imogen Heap shared every detail of the production of her album *Ellipse* on Twitter. Heap gained over a million twitter followers who shared her journey as she posted late into the night while working to finish the album. She also released the full vocal tracks to one of her songs on soundcloud.com for followers to add their own musical backing. Fans created over 500 versions and uploaded them to the site for others to hear.

Real pioneers in any field get there not just by studying but by experimenting and playing. Would you like to be recognised as a pioneer, a thought leader, a true original? Want to do something more than just rehash other people's ideas? Then make your life a laboratory. Test out new ways of doing things and notice what happens. What have you discovered to be true for you? What received wisdom have you found to be a load of hokum for you? Record it all as lab notes in your playbook. Take the problem you chose to help people with in the last chapter, throw out the rulebook, follow your hunches, and experiment with new ways of solving it. Report what you find and invite others to join the conversation. If you can come up with a new solution, this can be a speedy route to fame.

British time management guru Mark Forster is developing a radical new system called Autofocus to manage all your tasks using nothing more than a ruled notebook and a few simple instructions. He's experimenting with it in public and inviting others to try it out and feed back their findings in an online forum and social network. Although he didn't charge to take part, the payoff was a dramatic increase in website traffic. Visitors to his blog more than quadrupled, at one point topping 300,000 hits a month.

Myth 11: I must keep my good idea secret otherwise someone will steal it

Are you afraid to tell anyone the idea for your project or business in case someone steals it? Ideas are a lot less precious than you might imagine. There are very few totally original ideas: mostly they are just variations on a familiar format. Besides this, it's the execution that really matters. Think of the reality TV show *Big Brother*; if someone described it to you it wouldn't sound that exciting: 'We take a bunch of ordinary unknown people, put them in a house together and video everything they do for a couple of months.' It doesn't sound like something that became a prime-time hit in over 60 countries. That's because it's how it's actually executed that matters. The way you execute your idea will be uniquely yours. Someone else with a seemingly identical idea wouldn't produce the same final product because they don't, in reality, have exactly the same vision and approach.

The bottom line is that if you have great ideas, and the worst happens and someone steals your idea, you'll have more of them. The big problem with keeping your idea secret is that you lose the benefit of everyone else who could help you. I often meet people who say they can't tell me their business idea and it's frustrating because I would have been happy to give them a few minutes of free consultancy right there and then.

Just use common sense. If all you have is the idea right now and you don't have anything that ties the idea to you (e.g. the right contacts, industry knowledge, or specialist skills to make it happen), then use caution when talking with others who have more ability to execute it.

So are you ready to start playing the fame game? Here are the five steps to launch (or relaunch) yourself onto the world. Make it one of your play projects to implement these steps. If you are currently looking for employment rather than starting your own business, these strategies are still very relevant. In fact, following them may allow you to sidestep the whole, very limited, world of conventional recruitment and get noticed by someone who can help you create your ideal job. (More on this in Secret nine.)

Step one: Pimp your project

If you want to get known in the new crowded and noisy global marketplace, you have to dare to stand up and stand out. Find a way to juice things up. Don't become a fake, but a larger and louder version of yourself. If you're a young and hip IFA, you could brand yourself the rock 'n' roll financial adviser. If you're a calm voice of reason in a line of business where everyone sports designer jeans and an edgy haircut, get a pin-striped suit. Whichever it is, dare to be a maverick and break the accepted conventions of your field.

Colour outside the lines. Don't blend in; find a shocking or funny way to name or present your play project (or your whole business). Make it newsworthy; find the angle in what you do that makes it interesting, original or entertaining. The more remarkable you are, the less hard slog you have to put in to get yourself known.

Marketing is a tax you pay for being unremarkable.

Robert Stephens of tech support company Geek Squad

Sophie Boss on the chocolate effect

We called our business Beyond Chocolate because it was about not worrying about chocolate; beyond making it the enemy or this amazing thing that you shouldn't really have and should think of only from afar. But we could have called it Beyond Peanuts, Beyond Crisps, Beyond Mashed Potatoes, Beyond Anything. The point was to have a name that wasn't scary and that was media attractive. The fact that we had chocolate in the name of our business meant that the media came to us rather than us having to chase them. We eventually ended up being featured in The Daily Mail, The Independent on Sunday *and* The Observer.

Humour is a great tool to use throughout your work. Website onceivegone.com uses humour to lighten a very serious topic: communicating your wishes after your death. The registration page includes such questions as 'What do you intend to reincarnate as?' and 'Who would you like to haunt?'

Show your personality because people buy people, not just your services or products. Say what you really think. If you hate something that's common in your field, say so. Others will agree and will feel drawn to you as a result. Even those that don't will find your opinion interesting.

I work with many people first striking out on their own. And I am constantly amazed that when they launch their website or brochure, they take everything that makes them different, special, interesting, and talented and strip it out of their marketing! As a result, they end up with a website that looks exactly the same as everyone else's. This is not doing anyone a favour; how can a visitor to your site now tell whether they click with your personality and approach? Think of what's most striking about you – your friendliness, your cheeky sense of humour, your brilliant ideas, your obsession with detail – and build your entire brand around that. Show it in the text and styling of your marketing materials.

In this age, what's different about you, what's unusual about you is your greatest asset. Flaunt your quirks. Use your life experiences; we've all suffered setbacks, challenges and tragedies in our lives and often these are the events that have taught us the most. Use what you've learned.

All the marketing in the world won't help you unless you're doing good work. Live it and breathe it until you become great at it. You can only do that if you've chosen work you love. Build everything around your moment of magic and you'll attract people by word of mouth. Your marketing is then a matter of formalising the communication pathways for that good will. Be sure to communicate your passion for your work. The best marketing trick is to be crazy about what you're doing.

When you get this right, you'll find you start to get lucky. As long as you're out there doing the right work, you'll find you stumble across the right people and opportunities to help you move to the next stage. This is what I call 'engineering chance'. As long as you have your eyes open, you can take advantage of it.

When your energy is right, people and opportunities are attracted to you. When they show up, bill 'em.

Stuart Wilde, author of 18 books

A lot of people have negative associations with marketing, thinking it's about being disingenuous and conning people. It doesn't have to be. For people to enter any kind of relationship with you, whether personal or business, they need to know, like and trust you. Marketing at its best is simply a set of strategies to make this happen more easily.

One very useful tool for marketing your work is to be able to tell a good story about it.

The power of your story

Never underestimate the power of a good story about you, your art, project or business. It made Alex Tew a millionaire.

Back in 2005, Alex was a 21-year-old student about to begin a three-year Business Management course at the University of Nottingham. Alex was concerned that he would be left with a student loan that would take years to repay so he brainstormed ways to make some money on the internet to fund himself.

The idea he came up with was brilliantly simple. He decided to create a one-page website featuring a grid of 1,000 x 1,000 pixels which he would sell as advertising space. The cost was $1 per pixel and purchasers would buy them in 10×10 blocks to add their own logo or advert, with a link to their own website. If he sold all the pixels, it would make him a millionaire.

When MillionDollarHomepage.com launched on 26 August 2005, it became an internet phenomenon, at one point being ranked in the top 150 most visited websites in the world.

But what really made this website such a success? It was the story.

The story of how a young student facing debt made a million on the internet was one that hundreds of journalists around the world wanted to write about. The story appeared again and again in newspapers and magazines and on the web. And it's because that story got such exposure that so many people visited the website (which after all was not very exciting or pretty to look at!). And because so many people were visiting the website, everyone wanted to buy the pixels to advertise their products.

Alex sold every pixel and his final gross income was $1,037,100 – from a site that cost him 50 euros to create. It was a million-dollar story. What's your story?

Start a movement. When you feel strongly enough about what you're trying to do with your work, it becomes bigger than you – it becomes not just a business but a movement. What do you most want to change in your area of work? Take a stand on it and you'll attract a tribe of followers who support you. They will recruit other followers who can later become paying clients or customers.

Embrace your inner nerd. Players get passionate and even irate about their favourite topics whether it's bad typography, poorly roasted coffee beans or ill-fitting bras. The mainstream might find your obsession odd but the likelihood is that enough other people will share it and be attracted by your passion for it. This is true in a way it never was before if your business is on the web; even if you have a very narrow focus, you have the entire world in which to find the tribe of people who share your interest. Create your own 'global microbrand', as cartoonist and author Hugh Macleod calls it.

The Eden Project

The Eden Project in Cornwall has attracted over 11 million visitors since its construction. But when former songwriter and music producer Tim Smit first had the idea to turn a disused china clay pit in a remote part of England into the world's largest greenhouse, a lot of people said it could never work. I asked him how he knew it would.

I have known since my music business days that if you love something (and you are not a freak) there will be millions of people like you out there so the only issue is getting to them. This is the basis of great marketing. So, no, I never had doubts.

Step two: Choose your channel of communication

Your next step is to choose the channel (or channels) you will use to reach your fans, customers or clients. It has never been easier to reach an audience of people at little or no cost, launch your project, and build a community around it.

Would you like to have an audience of people eager to hear your latest news and ready to buy whatever you offer next? Your mid-to-long term aim must be to build an audience of people who have given you permission to contact them with your advice, ideas and news. Your ability to do this can make or break your mission to get paid to play. Just imagine you had a thousand fans subscribed to your newsletter or blog. That's a very useful thing when you come to releasing a new product, book or album. Send them a message announcing your new creation and you might sell some units straight away. And when you have ten thousand, it starts to get really interesting. It takes time to build a fanbase and, like compound interest on your savings, it takes time to pay off so start building it now.

There are now many channels you can use to reach people, from simple email to more interactive social media. Social media, such as Facebook, Twitter, YouTube, and blogging, is particularly useful for playing out your project. Some experts are now suggesting that any business not involved in social media will not survive in the long term. This might seem a bold claim, particularly if you currently consider Facebook and Twitter and so on to be an over-hyped waste of time. But I bet that you're already using social media even if you don't know it: you've read an Amazon review to help decide on a purchase, you've discovered a great YouTube video because it was linked from the one you were watching, or you've stumbled across a fascinating article that you didn't even realise was a blog post. And it's only just begun. Social media will be an integral part of every corner of the internet.

You can use social media to engage people, spread the word about what you do, get input and feedback, and even allow people to take your stuff and build on it in new ways. When you get it right, you'll find you can step out of the way and let people market you, your business, or your cause to each other.

Authenticity and integrity are the new currencies. Everyone knows what it's really like to work with you: from roofers to airlines, because the conversation about you is being held online in public. The growing trend is for real-time reviews: people tweeting or blogging while still at your conference or gig. You can't expect to short-change your customers and get away with it, as some large corporations have found out recently to their surprise. Smart companies are now replying to complaints with concern on Twitter. The trend is towards transparency. We can all follow the daily life of the Mayor of London, or the rockstar you couldn't get within 100 feet of before.

The question for you is, which channel do you want to use to play out your project? Read on to understand some of the best options.

Email

The first method people used to communicate with a mass of people on the internet was, of course, email. And it's still a very useful thing to have an email list of people interested in your work. To build one, use an online newsletter system to manage the database and send email newsletters (don't start cc'ing hundreds of people with your usual email program). The service should show you how to place a sign-up box on your website. Encourage your fans or potential customers to give you their email address in exchange for giving them something of value such as a useful how-to article. Every week or two, send an email to subscribers with something useful to them. When relevant, include a link at the end to something you offer. Make sure people can unsubscribe themselves whenever they want, and never add anyone to an email database without their permission – that's just rude.

While we're on the subject of email, a note about your own email address: Don't run your business on a free email address like hotmail – it looks unprofessional. It's best, in fact, not to use your email address from your Internet Service Provider either, because one day you might want to change provider and you'll lose the address. Instead, purchase your own domain name to use so that your email address becomes yourname@yourbusiness.com. (If you already have a domain for your website, set up your email on that.)

Read more about email marketing at ScrewWorkLetsPlay.com and start collecting email addresses today. You won't regret it.

Blogging

Blogging is a great tool for almost any project. It allows you to play out your idea and interact with your audience or customers. Sometimes it also leads to some great opportunities.

Grace Bonney set up her blog, Design Sponge, five years ago while still in her PR job. Now the website, which offers city shopping guides, recipes and craft ideas, is a full-time job for Bonney. She started on a free blogger.com page and now has 40,000 readers a day around the world. She has 13 freelancers and makes money from selling ad space.

Catherine Sanderson is author of the popular blog, Petite Anglaise, about a Brit's life in Paris. The blog came into existence on a whim one day, after reading the *Guardian*'s guide to weblogs. Minutes later, she'd created her own site using blogger. Her blog posts written while still in her secretarial job clinched her a book deal worth £400,000. Her second book, *French Kissing*, has just been published, yet she has said that 'If I hadn't started blogging, it would never have occurred to me that I could be a writer'.

Other bloggers who won book deals include Suzi Brent for her blog Nee Naw about her job as an emergency medical dispatcher in the London Ambulance Service and Gretchen Rubin's blog The Happiness Project on the year she spent test-driving all the theories (both old and new) on how to be happy. Julia Powell won not just a book deal but also a film deal from her blog The Julie/Julia Project, which chronicled her attempt to cook all the recipes in the classic cookbook *Mastering the Art of French Cooking*. The resulting book inspired the 2009 film *Julie and Julia* starring Amy Adams and Meryl Streep.

Of course, these examples are the exception. Most bloggers never achieve fame or make significant money from their blogs. Don't do it for the money, do it because you enjoy it (and ironically you'll be more likely to get famous as a result). But even if no one ever reads your blog except you and your mum, if you go through the process of writing ten posts over a month or two, your knowledge on your subject will have deepened, your writing will have improved and your thinking on your topic will have moved forward. And if you focus your blog on something interesting with a unique slant, you will find that others will want to follow you as you play with your topic.

Over 100,000 new blogs are created and a million or two blog posts published every single day. So how can you possibly write anything new? You don't need to. When you write in your own authentic voice, you are already unique. There is never going to be another exact copy of you with your talents, skills and experiences. If you create good content with your own style, you will attract the readers who resonate with it.

A blog is also a fast, easy alternative to creating your own website. In fact it's better than a boring static website that never changes. And it's possible in the best blogging systems like Wordpress to have a mix of blog and normal web pages so it can function as your main website too. This is far more preferable than having a website and a blog that are at different addresses and sending visitors to two different places. It's therefore my usual recommendation for anyone about to create their first website. To get started, go to a popular blogging site such as Wordpress.com and register for free. People who enjoy your blog posts can subscribe to get all future posts automatically in an RSS reader. Or use a service like Feedburner to allow people to get it delivered to their email inbox.

Does a blog sound like too much work?

Try something simpler like posterous (a simpler form of blog) or a tumblelog (a simple list of images, videos and quotes). Both of these are great for compiling images you like and writing short comments on them – ideal if you're exploring advertising, photography, or any form of design.

Facebook groups and fan pages can be used to build a community of like-minded people, share images, ideas and videos, and promote events. Or launch your own private social network with much of the same functionality completely for free at Ning.com. This means you can create a fully functioning private social network for your clan of Electronica fans or Labrador puppy owners where users can post pictures and videos, write their own blogs, and chat to each other.

Twitter is currently the hot topic of conversation in social media circles. It is billed as a micro-blogging system for 140-character messages. It's a great channel for sharing nuggets of advice, humour or gossip. It's the perfect place to share your expertise on your topic and engage others in conversation about it. Twitter users provided interview questions, case studies and interesting articles that have all contributed to the book you are reading now. (You can follow me on Twitter at @johnsw)

Alternatively you can just use Twitter to make people laugh. Justin Halpern moved in with his father at the age of 28. Not normally an indicator of imminent success, Justin turned it to his advantage.

His 73-year-old father's grumpy rants were so shocking and funny that he decided to share them with the world on Twitter. He tweets just one fragment of conversation from his Dad every day containing his frank and blunt observations on life. Justin now has over a million followers for @shitmydadsays, a book deal with a major publisher and a TV project planned with CBS.

Video

If speaking's more your style than writing, why not try videoing yourself? You can shoot videos using nothing more than the built-in webcam in your laptop or a £100 Flip Video camcorder. It's then just a couple of clicks to upload the results to YouTube for all to see.

Yes, people do get discovered for their comedy or song writing talents and go on to win record deals and TV appearances. But you can also use video as a way of promoting your business.

Tom Dickson, CEO of blender makers Blendtec, started WillIt-Blend.com, a series of videos blending unusual products to show off the power of their blenders. Blender experiments have so far included golf balls, lightbulbs, camcorders and an iPhone. The videos became a viral phenomenon and Tom has since appeared on national TV in America. As he reports, 'Within just a few short days, we had millions of views. The campaign took off almost instantly . . . Will it Blend has had an amazing impact to our commercial and our retail products.'

If you're camera shy, try an audio podcast instead. Record anything between 2 and 20 minutes of audio on your computer then upload it to your blog, submit it to iTunes, or use a free service like PodBean.com to do the whole process.

For every branch of the traditional media, there is now an online alternative that you can control yourself. Nothing now stands in the way between you and your fans. You don't need a broadcaster or publisher to give you permission to reach your audience. We own the media, let's use it. If you haven't checked recently, you will be stunned just what you can do in one afternoon using services on the net that are cheap or even free.

Publish your own book. Use print-on-demand sites like Lulu or Blurb to publish your own book. Upload your manuscript from your word processor, choose a cover and set a price to sell at. Now whenever someone wants a book, it is printed specially and delivered directly to them. And you keep the profit after the cost of production.

Host your own radio show. Open an account at blogtalkradio. com, give a talk, run a phone-in, or invite someone you admire to an interview. Let others listen in live on the web or access the recording later on your blog with a couple of clicks.

Launch your own TV station. Go to livestream.com or ustream.tv and choose a name for your channel. To fill your schedule, upload some videos from your hard disk or grab a bunch off YouTube. They'll run in a loop all day. Add your TV channel logo and insert titles at the bottom of the screen. Hit the transmit button and your station is live on the web around the world for anyone to watch. Plug in a video camera or just stand in front of your webcam and hit the 'On air' button to punch in and go live to your viewers.

Whatever you want to do, there's something out there to make it happen. Share your photos on Flickr or package them into beautiful photobooks on Blurb; share your music on MySpace and sell it on CD Baby; create an event and find attendees using Facebook events or Meetup.com; start your import business with an eBay shop. Open your own retail shop today: upload your designs to Cafépress or Zazzle and make them instantly available to buyers anywhere in the world as a T-shirt, mug, notebook, calendar or clock. If you handmake art or crafts, sell it on Etsy.com, the handmade marketplace. Whatever it is you want to do, you can now launch it in some form in one afternoon. What are you waiting for?

Decide the channel you will use to play out your project. If your head is now spinning with all the options, keep it simple and start a blog. You can always add other elements such as audio and video or Twitter updates later.

Step three: Who are your kind of people?

As you launch your project onto the world, think about who it is you most want to reach. Ultimately these people will be the ones who will pay you for what you do. When you're deciding what kind of customers, clients or fans you want to attract, your aim should be to market, sell to, and work with people you actually like.

Have you ever had the experience of trying to sell your services or products to someone you actually would rather not spend time with? I know I have. It rarely works and if you did actually win the sale, you've now entered a business relationship with someone you wouldn't choose to hang out with. When you look in your appointment diary, the reaction you should be having is, 'Great, I'm looking forward to seeing them tomorrow'.

Even if you're selling a product and won't have to speak to the customer again, it's still better to sell to people who are going to value what you do, get the most out of it and give you honest appreciative feedback, and avoid those that want to complain for the sake of complaining.

Think about who you would absolutely love to sell your services or products to. Most people think of demographics when asked this question – how old are they? What gender? What line of work? Or for those selling to organisations, what size of turnover? What industry? It's equally if not more important to think about psychographics: what are their values? What do they look for in a product? Do you want to sell to people who are down-to-earth and unpretentious or people who are trailblazers in the latest trends? Do you want people who appreciate the finer things in life or who love value for money? Think about these questions and note your responses in your playbook.

From all this, imagine your ideal client or customer. It could be someone you know or someone you would like to work with. Describe them in your playbook. If it's a particular person or organisation, grab a picture of them off the web and paste it into your playbook. When you are writing your blog or email newsletter, remember this ideal person you want to reach.

Does this mean you are ruling some people out? Isn't this a crazy way to run a business? Well, the truth is you're probably already appealing to a certain kind of client or customer already. All I'm suggesting is that you become more aware of it so that you can make sure the way you present and promote yourself is consistent.

What we're talking about here is niche marketing. Marketing your work is a bit like dating. You can't attract everyone; even George Clooney turns some women off. It's much better to find a small group of people who find you irresistible than a huge number of people who quite like you, because there's got to be a strong attraction for someone to take out their hard-earned money and hand it over to you.

It's much easier to grow your fame within a niche. It takes real time and effort to start to get known by people. It's easier, faster and cheaper to do it within a narrower section of society or business. And you can still offer a range of services or products to that niche.

I was at a networking meeting recently when a printer stood up to give his one-minute introduction to the room and said, 'I do all kinds of work for all people'. How much interest do you think this attracted? Not a lot. To come back to the dating analogy, if you are single and someone came up to you and said, 'Basically, I'm looking for a relationship with anybody at all', how attractive would you find it? It smacks of desperation. People prefer specialists. If you discovered someone whose entire business is aimed at solving exactly the problem you have right now, wouldn't you be interested in talking to them?

If you're just starting out, it may take time to discover your ideal client and your exact niche. Play it out and look for the patterns as you start to work with a variety of people and projects. If you've been working for yourself for a while already, think about which have been your favourite projects and who have been your favourite clients. Could you focus on winning more of these projects or clients?

If you're still worried about narrowing your focus, realise that you might not need a huge number of customers. If you provide a service and you're selling your time on a project basis you don't need the whole world to love you, just enough people to keep you in work. And that number might be a lot smaller than you imagine. A contractor who gets repeat business from clients can survive very well on just a handful of clients.

Even if you're an artist, musician, craftsperson or someone selling information products, you may be better off with a relatively small number of people that are crazy about you (and buy everything you offer) than a larger number of people that are only mildly interested in you.

Step four: Start the conversation

Once you've chosen your channel and know your people, how do you start? Your first blog post, email newsletter or video message could explain your angle on the topic you're going to be exploring. Write it in your own natural voice; there's no need to switch into formal business-speak. Keep it short. The shorter your writing or video, the more people will bother to read it or watch it. You'll see that the best bloggers sometimes write posts that are nothing more than an embedded video or a link with a sentence explaining why it's so interesting. Make a clear request at the end for feedback as comments or tweets.

Your job then is to keep yourself at the front of your fans' minds by keeping in touch with regular blog posts, tweets or email messages. This takes persistence and that's why it's so important you choose something you're genuinely interested in. I get people booking sessions with me two years after I first met them because they've been receiving my emails every month. What are the chances they would have remembered me without this?

Don't just send promotional messages. Send things of real value. There's enough spam and sales junk on the internet; add to the signal not to the noise. Send news, expert tips, engage your followers, canvass their opinions, offer to answer their questions online, run competitions. You might choose to directly address the problems you identified in the last chapter to work on. Ask people what their experience is of this problem and what solutions they've found. Or if you already know something that helps with this problem, explain it. You can also get some great content by interviewing interesting or well-known people in your field. Don't be afraid to give away your best ideas and content. Rather than losing you business, this will actually attract a lot more.

Once you have something for people to see, how do you get people to come look? This is a huge subject in itself but, to a certain extent, it will happen organically as you play out your passion for your topic. Things that increase the number of visitors to your blog or website include commenting on other people's blogs on a related topic; linking to other blog posts (which may be spotted by the owner of the blog concerned so that they come and read yours); having a hit video on YouTube; getting a link from a website with a lot of traffic; getting links from websites that Google considers important (thereby raising the deemed importance of your own site so that it appears higher up in searches); writing articles that include a link to your site and uploading them to repositories like ezine-articles.com; writing for other people's blogs and newsletters; and having your Twitter messages retweeted. Most of all, though, you must create good stuff that's worth the effort of reading or watching – and that takes practice, persistence and passion.

Step five: The art of seduction, or how to turn your fans into customers

Now you've started the conversation with the people you want to reach, how do you attract them towards buying your products or hiring you? Firstly, think from your reader's perspective when you're communicating with them. People starting out in business for themselves tend to talk about how they do their work or what features their products have but this is really not that interesting to the person looking to buy. They're more interested in the benefits or results they can expect from your service or product. But there's something even more powerful than this when you first want to get your readers' attention: it's to talk about the problems you identified them as having.

There's a famous phrase in advertising that says, 'Enter the conversation already going on in your customer's head'. Your customer or client's inner conversation is often about what's bugging them most: 'I've tried everything and I still can't get rid of this back pain', 'Why can't I find a TV that I can actually operate?', 'These mortgage payments are killing me', 'Why are all tie designs so boring?' When you write a blog post or email newsletter that addresses your readers' problems, you grab their attention.

Once you have their attention, don't try to convert your fans into buyers in one step. To return to our dating analogy, you can't really go up to someone who barely knows you and say, 'Hi, you look nice. Do you want to get married and have three kids?' Similarly in business, you shouldn't expect to convert strangers into buyers in one step. Instead, draw them step-by-step into a deeper relationship with you.

They might start by reading your blog, then giving their email address in exchange for a free guide you've created. If they like that, they might spend a little money with you to buy a small product or taster session. Some of the people that do that will go on to buy something more significant from you or hire you personally.

At each stage of this dance of seduction, make it clear what you want your quarry to do next; spell out what the next step is with a clear 'call to action'. When someone's read your website, what's the very next step you want them to take? Expecting them to pick up the phone might be too much of a jump; perhaps the best next step is to entice them to give you their email address so that you can put them on your mailing list. You can then send them an email that tells them about a free talk you are giving. Each step draws them closer into relationship with you.

Make it obvious what you want them to do. If you send out an email saying to get in contact, that's actually too vague. Do you want them to email you? Call you? End the email by putting the number right there: 'Call me on 0800 . . .'. You will be amazed how simple things like this will increase your success. My local independent cinema is currently raising funds for renovation. I ran into the manager who was brainstorming ways to find £140,000 within eight weeks. The first thing I did was look at the front page of their website. Where was the notice to ask people to donate? It was in tiny italicised writing buried in a small box of five recent news stories. He took my point and added a wide banner across the top of the website. If you want someone to do something, make it as easy as possible for them!

And finally, a note about coping with controversy

Listen to your own tastes. Be prepared to be unpopular.

Abraham Maslow, American psychologist, 1908–1970

Once you dare to take a stand and give up the anonymity of the crowd, don't be surprised if you piss some people off. In fact if this doesn't happen, you're probably playing it too safe (particularly if you're trying to change the status quo). Remember that to turn some people on, you have to turn other people off. As long as you are an amorphous blob, no one can take offence; once you define yourself, you will polarise people for you or against you.

Ray Charles once said his mother gave him two excellent pieces of advice: 'Always be yourself' and 'Not everyone is gonna like you'. It really doesn't matter what your topic is or which stand you take, someone won't like it. I've seen people angrily attack others on topics as diverse as stone masonry, knitting, and how to be happy. No one is immune, so accept that it's part of the life of being a player.

Everyone has the right to disagree with you. What's more troubling is when someone turns that into a personal attack on you. Remember that if the strength of someone's reaction seems to be wildly out of proportion to what you did, then accept that it is not actually about you and what you said. It's more likely that you've triggered their emotional baggage.

If someone makes an unpleasant personal attack on you, the best response might be to ignore it. Avoid getting drawn into any kind of argument or justification. What you give your energy to tends to grow – don't give it to conflict. There is a danger for all of us that the negative responses get stuck in our head while all the positive feedback passes us by. Start to do the opposite by collecting all the appreciations, encouraging comments and good reviews that come your way.

Now you know how to start to attract your own fanbase, in the next chapter you'll find out how to offer them something irresistible.

Put it into play

Keys to this secret:

➡ Pimp your project – dare to stand out.

➡ Embrace the new channels of communication to reach your audience.

➡ Describe your ideal client or customer.

➡ Start the conversation and keep in touch.

➡ Attract your fans towards becoming paying customers.

What you should have now:

➡ a chosen channel to start communicating;

➡ a description of your ideal client or customer;

➡ some ideas of how to start the conversation.

Take ten minutes to play:

➡ Go and sign up for a blog, Twitter account or email newsletter service.

➡ If you already have one, start crafting a post or message to send as described in Step four.

Exclusive extras on ScrewWorkLetsPlay.com

➡ more about blogs, social media and email marketing: which services to use, how to sign up for them and use them;

➡ links to some of the best blogs on the web.

Secret seven
How to create an irresistible offer

The companies that survive longest are the ones that work out what they uniquely can give to the world, not just through growth or money but their excellence, their respect for others, or their ability to make people happy. Some call those things a soul.

Charles Handy, management expert and author

You've now seen how to use the latest online systems to get yourself known for what you do. You've also seen how to define the people you want to be known by. The question now is, what will you offer them? We looked earlier at how important it is to know the problems you want to help people with. This chapter will help you work out what solution you can provide for those problems and what form to deliver it in. Once you know that, you'll have something to offer that allows you to get paid to play. Here's an example from UK-based business The Money Gym.

The Money Gym – making millionaires

The Money Gym is a business started in 1999 by Nicola Cairncross and later joined by business partner Judith Morgan. As Nicola explains, The Money Gym

> *teaches ordinary people about money in property, shares, internet and business. This includes how money works, how to become financially free and self-reliant, how to get out of the day job, create financial integrity now and financial security for the future.*

When I first had the idea, I was already wealth coaching under my own name but wanted to tie it all together into a one year programme, and involve the clients with each other too. I also wanted to create a name that said what it did on the tin and was not linked to me specifically, so that I might be able to sell it one day if I wanted to.

As soon as I had the idea, I immediately wrote the sales letter describing the offer (very good for getting clear about what you are offering, to whom, and what the benefits are), I set up the Join Now button on the shopping cart, and sent it all out as an email while I went to pick the kids up from school. I gave away the first 5 spaces in the one year programme to the first 5 applicants off the block, and when I got back, an hour or so later, I had 27 new clients!!

The problem we often talk about helping with is, 'you might be earning well, but if you stop working, does the money stop as well?'. As many of our members are women they also seem to be very concerned with their independence, in that they don't want to feel dependent on men for their financial security. And there is much concern, with pensions underperforming, of a potentially impoverished retirement.

Our solution is to assess each client, help them create a plan, and then put it into action, based on their starting point, existing assets and skills/abilities. For our clients it's a three step process; of getting financial control, then making more money to invest (and to create an improved quality of life), and then of becoming financially free.

The Money Gym now has well over 1,000 members paying between £27.50 and £479.50 a month depending on their membership level. Over the years, Nicola says, 'we've helped create at least 20 millionaires and helped many others become financially free so they only work if they want to. And both Judith and I absolutely love what we do!'

Find out more about The Money Gym at *themoneygym.com*

Getting paid to play means doing something you really enjoy while providing something people are happy to pay for. Your job now is to find something you can offer that people really want. And what people really want are solutions to their problems. Look back at the list of problems you wrote down in Secret five. What can you offer that solves these problems or at least goes some way towards helping with them? What results can you promise for people who have this problem? Remember that it's the results people are really paying for when they buy your product or service.

People don't want to buy a quarter-inch drill. They want a quarter-inch hole!

Theodore Levitt, Harvard Business School marketing professor

The clearer you can get on the results you provide, the easier it will be to get paid for them. Here are some examples. If you're a virtual assistant helping clients with the problem of being too busy to organise their business appointments and sales meetings, you could solve it by doing all of it for them. The result for your clients could be more business – and more money coming in.

If you're a hypnotherapist you could address the common problem of fear of flying. The result for the client is that they can finally travel further afield to warmer holiday destinations, enjoy the journey, and arrive already relaxed.

If you run a blog about Bali-inspired interior design and you import related crafts and furniture, you can solve the problem for people who love the Bali style but don't know how to create it in their own home. The result for your readers and customers could be a beautiful lounge or bedroom featuring some of your unique pieces not found anywhere else in the West.

The more significant your results and the more impact you have on the problem, the more valuable you are. And the more valuable you are, the more you can get paid. If the problem you address is boredom at work, you can have a small impact, like making people laugh for a few minutes with a funny blog – in which case you might make a fraction of a penny per person off advertising. Or you can provide someone a complete out-of-the-box business opportunity to allow them to escape their job altogether – in which case you can charge hundreds or thousands of pounds.

Once you know what the results are that you provide, the question then is how do you deliver them? You could provide your results by offering a physical product, a printed book, or an online information source, or you might do it by working with the client directly. You can provide a similar result in lots of different ways. The Money Gym, for example, provide their expertise as a printed book, an online home study course and face-to-face coaching, with very different prices. Different people will choose different methods of delivery.

Here are some simple ways of delivering the results you're interested in providing. None of these have the hassle of running a full-blown business requiring staff and premises or a large financial investment. Even if you're currently looking to find another job rather than go self-employed, you might find that experimenting with one of these channels helps you to create your next role (we'll look at this in greater depth in a later chapter).

Providing a service

A lot of people start their journey into self-employment by providing a service to individuals, groups or organisations and charging for it by the hour, day, week or project.

People who charge by the hour include counsellors, life coaches, complementary therapists, accountants and plumbers. Contractors and consultants often charge by the day. Others such as web designers and computer programmers might charge by the project. There are now some people who charge by the minute and websites like Greatvine.com and LivePerson.com exist to help you do exactly that.

To get known, practise the steps laid out in Secret six 'How to play the fame game'. Share your thoughts about your field of expertise on your blog, Twitter or other channel as described. This allows potential clients to understand your perspective and approach.

Advantages: If you have the skill, this can be the fastest way to turn your value into money. There is no complex business plan to write, no premises or systems to organise. It can be a good place to start because it puts you in direct contact with your target market so you get a sense of what's on their mind, what their problems are and what they want. This knowledge can support you in later creating a product or business to deliver the same results without needing to work with them directly. If you have specialist skills that are in high demand, you can earn a good income compared to similar people in a job. With a high enough rate, you can afford to take some time off in between projects.

Disadvantages: Selling your time is like running on a hamster wheel: you can get going straight away; the money's fine while you're working but as soon as you stop, the money's gone. Also, it can be difficult to find time to win your next client while you are on a project. It can end up feeling pretty much like a job. When you factor in unpaid holidays, sick leave, training time and times when you can't find any work, you find your annual income is not as great as it first appeared. And if you want to get really rich, this is not a good route because you only have a limited number of hours per month you can charge out. You won't see anyone in the annual rich lists who sells their time.

Ways to make it work for you

Here is a great tip if you're going to sell your time by the hour. If you sell every hour individually, you may end up talking to a prospective client for 30 minutes to sell them one hour of your time. Instead, package a number of hours into a solution and add in other items like physical products or information products. For example, a massage therapist, rather than selling a one-hour massage for £50, can sell the 'Ultimate relaxation package' of three massages, a relaxation CD, a printed guide to destressing your life, and some relaxing bath oil to use at home – all for £170. Not everyone will go for it, but some will buy it just as readily as the one-hour offering. Productising your services in this way can make them much easier to sell, particularly if you can clearly quantify the results a client can expect from it.

When working on a project basis, if you can charge enough for your time, you can start to take time off between engagements. Rather than 'Time is money', this means 'Money is time'; the more you charge, the more time you can take off. If you can earn four times your living expenses, then for every month worked you can take three months off to do other things – go travelling, write your novel, record an album.

Some people work this model very well. There are IT contractors who do a six-month contract and then take six months off to travel the world. Ultimately, if you do not enjoy the paid work then you are not getting paid to play. You simply end up dreading your return to work! Worse than this, you have to spend some of your time off marketing and selling yourself into work you don't really want. Remember the aim is to find a supporting income stream that is enjoyable.

Consultancy

Consultants are hired for their specialist expertise for short durations of a few days to a few months. They often charge by the day and can be paid £1,000 a day or even more. My experience of being an independent consultant is that although people hired me for my specialist expertise, many times that expertise simply allowed me to understand their language and their business. A lot of what I provided was actually common sense. I would ask people what was going wrong, what they thought would work better and write it all up in a report. The answers to a company's problems are often available right there within the company itself, so don't imagine you always need to bring some radical new insight.

It's not always the most skilled person who gets the work. Never underestimate the value of simply being around at the right time and being a likable and reliable person to work with. I've been hired purely, as someone explained, because 'I know you'll do the work on time' (even if they didn't know that I worked late into the night to finish it).

If you have a good level of expertise in an industry and you would enjoy being involved with cutting-edge projects, start going to conferences and networking events and meet people who could hire you. 'Consultant' is a very broad label; it really pays to know the problems you help with and the solutions you can provide so you can communicate just what you do for clients. A good way to start is to fill a recognised role like project manager or technical architect.

A good play project for you if you're looking to move into consultancy is to write a white paper – an article demonstrating cutting-edge thought on a current hot topic.

Now for some really exciting stuff. How would you like to be able to make some of your income without having to turn up at all?

How to make money in your sleep – or the wonders of passive income

If you've spent your whole life turning up somewhere in order to get paid, it can be a dramatic shift to start thinking about getting paid without being there. Passive income is income from a project that once you've set it up, keeps paying you without any further work – think of royalties on a book or a song you've written. We'll look at several more modern ways to create your first passive income in a moment.

When you earn your first piece of income without being present, it is quite a thrill. I remember waking up one morning to read an email telling me that that while I was asleep someone had paid £15 for a downloadable audio recording from my website. The recording had already been automatically delivered to the buyer without me needing to do anything. It's a small sum, but it was without doubt the best £15 I have ever earned. (Fortunately the amounts have grown somewhat since then!)

Passive income is a subject of much hype. In reality, almost no income is 100 per cent passive. When you've written your book, you have to promote it. Even if you own a property to let out and have an agency manage the tenants, you will still occasionally have to talk to them when something unexpected comes up. I prefer to call this 'low-maintenance income' but I'd take this any day instead of turning up to the same place to do the same thing day in, day out. It's also a great way to support yourself while doing something that might not pay (e.g. your art, writing or travel).

The internet is probably the easiest and lowest-risk way of creating a low-maintenance income stream. Here are four ways to get started.

1. Information products – the new way to sell your expertise

If you have a good level of expertise in any subject and a knack for sharing it, there are now a multitude of ways to make money without turning up. They all use the internet as your broadcast channel and the vehicle is information products. An info-product is simply your expertise captured as text, audio, video or graphics distributed in a number of possible formats – ebook, MP3, video file, video broadcast or teleconference class.

The wonderful thing about information products is that they cost almost nothing to produce and distribute: they purely require your time. This means you get close to a 100 per cent profit margin. Not only that but, also, because they are specialised to address a small niche of people, they can often be sold for considerably more than a physical book or CD! When you consider that you might only make 50 pence from a traditional book sold through a publisher, earning £10 or more from an ebook suddenly looks very appealing. And many information products are sold at ten times that price. This makes info-products far more appealing to offer than physical products which carry the problems of manufacture and distribution.

What kind of subject can you write an info-product on? Anything a large number of people have a problem with. Look back at your list of problems you want to help with and make the content of your info-product how to solve one of them.

To make it pay, you need a large number of people to tell about your product. This means a large list of email addresses of people interested in your topic, or a lot of website traffic, or a mass of followers on social media. The previous chapter showed you how to create this but if you don't have a large list of followers yet, you can do a deal with people who do and pay them commission on sales. For instance, approach someone who has an email list of several thousand people who are likely to be interested in what you offer (people who are similar to your picture of an ideal client) and ask them to email their database offering your information product. You then pay them up to 50 per cent commission on the resulting sales.

There's a lot of 'get rich quick' hype on the web about info-products. The truth is that creating one of real value takes time and effort.

Persuading people to buy it requires expertise too. Info-products are, however, a great addition to your other income streams. If you are an established hypnotherapist, a downloadable relaxation recording might be a good addition and a nice introduction to your style of working for people who might go on to have a session with you.

Don't consider yourself an expert?

You don't even need to be an expert to create information products. If you have a passion for a topic and an angle you want to explore, you can create valuable and high-profile content simply by interviewing people who are recognised experts. Interviewees will usually give their time for free because it helps promote their other work.

Some internet marketers have simply identified a specific problem people have and then hired someone else to write an ebook about it.

The power of knowing the problem

Daniel Wagner is now a recognised expert in internet marketing and yet it wasn't that long ago that he was a novice himself, as he explains here.

In 2006 I did some simple research on the Internet (that I could show anyone how to do in 10 minutes) and discovered that dog training was a great market to create information products for. Now just to make it clear, I don't have a dog, I know nothing about dogs, I don't actually like dogs. But I knew from my very simple research that it would be a market that I can make money from.

So I set up a one page website to ask that market of dog owners a simple question, 'What is the most pressing question about dog training that you need answering right now?' Once I had the answers, I hired someone else (who knew the topic) for $500 to *write the ebook to answer those questions. Within 3 months, I made more than $23,000 in sales in a market I had no knowledge of, didn't know anybody, had no expertise in; and I keep now, still to this day, this is 3 years later, making money from this market by offering new things to people who are interested in dog training.*

I have since built over 27 money-producing websites for myself and over 100 information products as e-Books, audio interviews, DVDs and online video. And I have helped over 600 people to do what I did.

Find out more about Daniel Wagner's work on his blog *danielwagner.com*

Simple ways to create an information product

Info-products come in many different forms. Here are a couple of simple ways to make one.

Ebooks – write out your expertise on a subject in a word processor and convert it into an Adobe PDF file for easy download. You can then sell it on your website or place it in a repository like clickbank. com which provides the ordering system for you. Ebooks typically sell for anywhere between £10 and £50 depending on the topic, the amount of content and any additional elements such as downloadable recordings.

Audio recordings – downloadable interviews, audio classes and so on usually in MP3 format. Two of the easiest ways to make them are to interview an expert and record it (or have someone interview you about your expertise), or run a teleclass and record it. A teleclass is a teleconference call with you and your participants (perhaps 10–20 people or more) on a conference line. Talk on your subject of expertise for 20 minutes then take questions from people. You might charge a small amount for people to take part in the teleclass, or provide it for free to prospective customers. You can then give away the recording, sell it on its own, or include it in a larger package of products. Always warn people in advance if they are taking part in a recording of any kind.

2. Affiliate marketing – or how to sell a product without having to make it

If you don't have a product of your own, you can now make money by promoting other people's products and receive a commission payment every time someone buys one. There are people who make a good living just doing this. If you're in the habit of recommending other people's good stuff anyway, why not take the commission they're offering? Sounds good, huh? A lot of people seem to think so. As a result there is a lot of competition out there for affiliate marketers so, just like anything else, you'll need to become good at the skills required – online advertising (to attract website traffic), copywriting to describe the product, and choosing the right products to offer. But if you like fiddling around on the internet, it can be fun to learn it all. And the skills are useful for marketing your other streams of income too. Affiliate marketing can be a great addition to your other lines of work.

When you see a product that helps with the problems you are addressing for people, look for a link to 'Our affiliate programme' or similar. Often you can join immediately by filling in a simple form. You are then given a unique link to that product. Send an email or write a blog post explaining why you recommend it and include your unique affiliate link. When someone clicks on it to buy the product, you will automatically earn the commission, usually paid by PayPal.

You can go a step further and use an affiliate portal like Commission Junction or Affiliate Window. When you register with these sites, you can then search for any kind of product you want to promote, join as an affiliate very easily and start promoting their products. This includes services and physical products from big name chains.

3. Blogging

As we saw in Secret six 'How to play the fame game', there are many reasons to get into blogging – it's a way to play out your ideas and it's a great marketing tool. And, yes, it can even directly make you money. Very few bloggers make a significant income directly from their blogs because you need a huge number of readers to make it pay, but it's worth understanding as part of a larger business strategy.

Blogs are monetised in a combination of ways: with affiliate marketing (as we've just seen), by showing adverts (using a service like Google Adwords), by promoting and selling your own info-products, or by turning your blog into a membership site as we'll see next.

4. Membership programmes

A membership (or continuation) programme is any income stream where you charge customers at regular intervals, usually monthly or annually. In return, you provide useful information, training and support on your topic of expertise. This could on be how to train dogs, how to change career, how to set up your first online shop and so on. Membership programmes give you the chance to have a deeper and longer-term connection with your customers. Sometimes they operate as a community around a common interest. Fans of American TV and film director David Lynch, for example, can join his own membership site at DavidLynch.com offering exclusive access to his film, art, music and animation projects for $10 a month. Or membership programmes can be built around a common problem or goal, as in the case of The Money Gym that we saw earlier.

Membership programmes are exciting as a business model because once you've convinced someone of the value of being a member, they keep paying you until they actively unsubscribe. Imagine you charge £10 a month, and in return you provide a training video, teleclass or downloadable audio. If you can attract a hundred members, that's £1,000 a month of revenue. Find 500 and you're making £5,000 a month. Many people charge a lot more than £10. (Charge £21 a month and if you manage to get 2000 members, you'll make a million pounds a year!) As ever, you need to provide great value, be able to attract a lot of potential customers, and then effectively communicate the results members can expect so that they want to join. Fortunately, these are all things you can learn in the course of your play projects.

A membership site can grow out of a blog. If you can write valuable content regularly, and start to attract a good number of readers, you are in a good position to create exclusive membership content and start to charge for it. If you don't have enough content or expertise yourself, you can partner with someone who does.

Advantages: The great advantage of these passive income streams is the ability to do the work once and get paid repeatedly for it. They are a great addition to other things you might offer, such as hourly sessions or consulting time. They are also a great way to build a product funnel: a range of things to offer from free to the low-priced to the most expensive. This allows people to get a taste of your work at a low price and decide whether to move on to buying something more expensive.

Disadvantages: Creating a good info-product takes time and it's all too easy to put it off while you focus on earning money in the here and now. Make it a play project to find the easiest and most natural way for you to create your first info-product; perhaps recording a talk or workshop you are already committed to delivering. Or take something you've written for another purpose and expand on it to make an ebook.

There is more on all these strategies at ScrewWorkLetsPlay.com.

Other ways to deliver your solution

There are lots of other ways you can deliver solutions to people's problems: you can invent a product design and license it for manufacture; you can self-publish a book; run events and workshops; sell your photos to a stock library; create a software application (or hire someone to do it on elance.com or rentacoder.com) and sell it on the web; or you can develop an online service which charges for usage or makes money through advertising. Whatever it is, find a way to play it out, experiment with it, and use the techniques in Secret four 'How to guarantee your success' to ask advice from people who know the specific challenges and strategies of this kind of project.

Remember from the principles of Wealth Dynamics in Secret two that you don't have to provide everything yourself. If you enjoy marketing, or editing, or building websites, you can do this for other people's products and services rather than create your own. You can team up with someone who has good content or has very different skills and create something together.

You now have the basic formula for getting paid to play: if you can deliver a great solution to a pressing problem and do so at a price people are happy to pay, you will have created an irresistible offer. In the next chapter we'll look at how to launch your offer onto the world and win your first playcheque.

Put it into play

Keys to this secret:

➡ Know the results you want to create for people.

➡ Choose a way to deliver to those results: freelancing, consulting, information product, membership programme, and so on.

What you should have now:

➡ something to offer the people you most want to work with.

Take ten minutes to play:

➡ Start writing something that describes your offer (often referred to as a sales letter): describe the problem you address, the results you provide, how you deliver those results, and why you are capable of doing this – your training, experience, and any testimonials to back you up. Also think about how much you want to charge for it.

➡ Arrange to show this to potential customers/clients and get some feedback. Once it looks good enough, place it on your website or in your brochure.

Exclusive extras on ScrewWorkLetsPlay.com

➡ more about offering services like freelancing and consulting;

➡ more on how to generate passive income, create information products, become an affiliate marketer, and launch a membership site.

Secret eight
How to win your first paycheque

The secret of living is to find people who will pay you money to do what you would pay to do – if you had the money.

Sarah Caldwell 1924–2006, Opera conductor and founder of the Boston Opera Group

You've now seen how to use the latest online systems to get yourself known and how to offer something that people really want. Now it's time to put it all into practice and actually make some money. This chapter will show you how to win your first paycheque and prove you can get paid to play. Remember that being a player means that you are creating your work; there is no job for someone to hand you; no standard formula to getting paid. But if you are determined, persistent, and willing to think creatively, there will be a way to get the experience you want from your work. Here's how schoolteacher Robert Chalmers made his transition to getting paid to play.

From school teaching to show business

Eight years ago music teacher Robert Chalmers decided it was time for a change: 'I realised that whilst teaching was incredibly rewarding it was incredibly hard work and relentless. The paper work element of the job was beginning to cloud my enjoyment. I was beginning to become bored. I was Head of Department – I achieved my goal – I didn't want to progress further up the teaching career ladder – that didn't interest me. So that was it for me – I would be doing the same job for the rest of my life until I retired – and probably at the same school! That seriously frightened me. What would I have achieved in my life? I wanted to work in show business but that was a dream, not a reality; but then why have dreams if you're not going to follow them.

With the support and encouragement of my wife I decided that I would hand in my notice at the end of the next academic year. I would take a chance – my wife was working – we would have to make cut backs – but we could do it.'

All he needed was his first break . . .

'After writing to well over 300 theatre producers, theatre houses and musical directors I got a call from Linda Edwards at The Landor Theatre (a fringe theatre venue above a pub in Clapham, London) saying they were looking for a musical director for a show they were putting on because they had had a cancellation from a previous show. It was a "profit-share" show. We only got paid if the venue made any profit. The theatre seats 60 people maximum. The show was *Side By Side by Sondheim*; a cast of five and me at the piano. It was the most scary and yet exhilarating thing I had done for a long time.'

His advice to others looking to leap? 'You have to be strong. Don't expect things to happen over-night. Family support is vital. It is scary – small things will lead on to bigger and better things. Be prepared to be patient.'

It certainly worked for Robert: 'Four years later I found myself in Belfast conducting *Mamma Mia!* in front of 3,500 people at the Odyssey Arena. As I walked out to the orchestra pit from backstage to a packed arena with an audience raring for the show to start, that's the time when I thought "Wow – I've made it!" '

And now he's worked as musical director on shows all over the UK including *Joseph and the Amazing Technicolor Dreamcoat*, *Blood Brothers*, *Full Monty*, *Our House*, and *Fame*, as well as the international tour of *Mamma Mia!*

You don't have to try to get paid for every play project you undertake; you can of course carve some time out of your leisure time for some of them. But if you're reading this book, you ultimately want to do more than just create a hobby crammed into the spare time smeared around your day job. Getting paid for your playing means you can do more of it, and you can start to tip the balance away from the work you don't enjoy to the things that feel like play. Money makes play sustainable – it allows you to keep playing.

As comedian Eddie Izzard says, 'I'm not a capitalist, I am a creativist. I want to make money so that I can create things.' As long as you are getting paid for something other than your play project (e.g. a day job), you will always be splitting your time, attention and energy.

As soon as we start talking about money, you might be tempted to get all serious and 'practical' and make some terrible compromises in your choice of project. This is the problem with the whole area of work – we've been trained to take whatever we can get when this really isn't necessary any more.

You know you're on the right track when you would do the central part of your work for free because it is so much fun. We looked at what this is for you in Secret one. If you can solve problems for people while doing this, there will be a way to monetise it, that is, make an income.

Myth 12: You can't get paid for doing what you love

A lot of people believe the myth that you simply can't get paid for doing what you love – despite the fact that people all over the world do just that. Whatever it is that you'd like to do, you can bet that someone somewhere in the world makes their living out of doing exactly that. Some things of course are more competitive or take longer to get established. If you want to write a best-selling novel or become a famous architect, you have a long journey ahead of you.

▶

Here's the thing though: if you choose the right path, you'll enjoy the journey. What this means is that as soon as you start, you've already arrived; you're a success. Being a success is really just finding a sustainable way to do something you love and really care about. To become a success, do those things that feel like play in a way that solves problems for people and find a way to monetise the value you provide.

If you have the habit of dabbling with lots of possible money-making ideas and never following them through to the final step to actually make a return, then it's time to do something different. Take your project all the way to the point where you can sell it at least once. The income may only be small but it's an important symbol of your ability to turn something you've created into real money.

But I need some money right now!

Making money from a completely new line of work is likely to take some time. During your transition, you'll probably need another source of income. If you're currently in a job you're keen to get out of, do pause for a moment and check whether you can give your job a makeover to make it more enjoyable while you're creating a new line of work elsewhere.

My client Susan decided after a number of sessions that it would be best for her to stay in her current job a little longer. We had been working on how to find something more creative for her. I asked, 'Have you told your boss the kind of work you really want to do?' and she admitted she hadn't. The next day she spoke to her boss and explained she wanted more work using her creative writing and sense of design. Her boss said, 'That's great, we need someone to work on the brochures and the website, would that suit?' Susan was delighted.

Can you give your current job a makeover in a way that makes it a better fit while you find something completely new? Can you take on new responsibilities that will help you when you finally do escape to something else? Can you go part-time while you transition?

If you're already self-employed, the quickest way to make some income is to look at something that you can do that you're already qualified for and experienced in. The problem is you might find that you suddenly can't seem to get the work you used to do. I've experienced this myself and I often see it in my work with clients. They decide they'll do one more contract or temp job to bolster their bank balance before they quit for good but strangely can't seem to get it. Why? Because once you've lost your enthusiasm and you've psychologically moved on, somehow people can just pick it up – even when you try your hardest to appear keen. You just can't fake enthusiasm. And if you try, you'll find yourself competing against someone else who genuinely wants the work. Guess who'll get it?

Even if this is an area of work you're looking to escape eventually, take a moment to look for a piece of it that is most appealing. What's your favourite kind of project or role in this area? Focus your search for income in this area. Your enthusiasm will help you win it and it'll be more enjoyable when you do. Alternatively, if you know you can survive for 6–12 months without much income, perhaps it's time to cut your losses and start building your new life.

Winning your first playcheque

Earning your very first income for doing something you love is an important landmark; it's your first *playcheque*. You may find it takes more effort to get your first sale than for the next ten added together. Or you may find it drops in your lap seemingly without effort.

If you possibly can, win your first playcheque while still in your current work. This means you're still being paid during the first few months when you might not be making much from your play yet. This has the added advantage that you will have less of the air of desperation about you compared with the person who needs the new income to survive.

Getting paid for your play project is the best way to prove its value to others. It's a very basic but genuine form of market-testing.

Myth 13: All my friends have said they would buy what I'm offering, so I must be on the right track

Asking your friends if they'd buy what you're offering is not market-testing. Getting paid is a far better test that you are on the right track than the positive comments of your family and friends. It's important to have the encouragement of those nearest to you but it's not the basis for a business. The only real test for whether people will buy something is to sell it to them – and at the actual price you will need to charge for it to make you a living. People will say all sorts of nice things about how they would buy what you're creating but unless they reach for their wallet and hand you their money for it, it's not enough.

It's appropriate that you might start out by charging less when you have limited experience or your product is still in rough form, but you need to know that there is a way further down the line to make the money you need.

A note about free

When you're just starting out, it's no bad thing to do some work for free. If you have a chance to go do exactly what you love most and get better at it in the process, do so. Any opportunity early on to experience being in flow, doing that thing you were born to do, is worth taking. Look for a fair exchange of value; it doesn't have to be money. If someone offers you a chance to demonstrate your skill in front of a large audience of prospective customers, this can be a great marketing opportunity. You might give a free talk at a conference or write an article for a magazine. The results from this kind of exposure can be more effective than paid advertising – and all it costs is your time.

If you're continuing to work for free because you're afraid of charging properly, it's time to bite the bullet and get professional. Providing something for free does not constitute market-testing; everyone likes free! Even if you're still training in the skill you are practising, it's a good discipline to charge at least a token amount. This puts things on a professional footing. Also, people don't value things that are free. The drop-out rate for free events for instance is huge – 60 per cent or even greater. Charging even a small amount dramatically increases people's commitment so that they are more likely to turn up – and to do so on time!

Myth 14: I can't possibly charge for what I'm doing yet – I need to read more books and take more courses and workshops

This myth is often just fear in disguise. Books, workshops and train-ing courses are great to build your skills and keep you motivated but don't use them as an excuse not to get started. Start small and don't overpromise.

Run a campaign

To win your first playcheque, run a campaign. This works really well if you're aiming to land a job or sell your services as a free-lancer, consultant or independent professional but it can also be modified to help you win your first large product order or your first agent, reseller or supplier. If what you're selling is one of the online passive income models described in the previous chapter such as an information product, your campaign is most likely to find someone who will promote your product for you.

Say you want to launch yourself as a web designer or virtual assistant or you want to sell your homemade cosmetics or foodstuff to a supermarket. Your first step is to have a clear offer as we saw in the last chapter (Secret seven) and to know your ideal client or customer as we discovered in Secret six. Then make it a play project to throw all your energy and effort into getting exactly the work you want to do with the people you want to work with. This is not the time to make wild compromises. Don't assume that by spreading your net wider you improve your chances. You don't. By spreading your focus, you weaken the effect. Compare a laser to a floodlight. They are equally bright but the laser focuses all its power into a tiny point. This gives it the strength to cut through paper and even metal. When you focus a lot of energy in a single place, you'll be surprised just what you can achieve.

My escape from the world of jobs

My early career was in technology innovation for the broadcast industry. When I first chose to become an independent consultant, I decided I would like to work for the BBC. They seemed to be doing the most interesting work in my area; I liked the friendly people I had met there; it was the best-known broadcaster in the world (I like to work for the best) and it had been something of a childhood dream of mine to work for them.

While still in my job, I called everyone I knew who worked in or around the BBC. I also called all my colleagues in the rest of the industry and asked them if they knew of anyone inside the BBC who might be able to hire me. I emailed all the people that might be able to help that I had email addresses for. I read the latest news on the projects the BBC were running and sometimes cold-called people who were mentioned in the news reports.

And after three months . . . absolutely nothing happened! I had now left my job with nothing else on the horizon. Finally one morning while I was still in bed, I got a call on my mobile phone, 'Hi. I'm calling from a division of the BBC, can you come in for an interview today?' I started my first contract the following Monday.

When you're starting out on your own, it can sometimes take months of pushing before you get noticed. As long as you are getting encouraging responses from the people you talk to, don't be surprised if it looks like nothing is happening in the meantime.

Notice the feedback you're getting and be willing to fine-tune your campaign according to the response you get. Be ready for the fact that even with the best planning in the world, taking expert advice, and following your own instincts, your grand launch into a new line of work sometimes falls flat on its face on its first attempt. It's what you do next that will determine your success; will you give up or make some changes and try again?

Here's how to run your own campaign

Get clear what you'd like. Be specific enough to land an opportunity you will enjoy but not so specific that you make it near impossible to find it.

Back when I was working as a programmer on special effects software, I went on a careers workshop and a couple of people there asked me to help them find work in my company. A woman called Sarah said, 'Can you ask at your company if there is any work going?' I asked what work and she said, 'Anything at all'. A second person, David, told me he wanted to be a special effects artist and asked if I could ask around at work for someone who could give him some advice.

Who do you think I could help the most? Sarah's request was so vague I didn't know what to do with it. David's request was easier to deal with because it was more specific. I went and spoke to some of the people at work involved in the special effects industry and asked their advice which I then passed back to David. When you're asking for help, keep your questions specific.

Write your killer email

Write an email covering:

➡ what you're looking to do and who for: if you're working for yourself rather than going for a job, this is where knowing the problem you solve and what solution you are offering is very helpful;

➡ what you bring that is of value to the people who will hire you (skills, knowledge, experience, any previous high-profile clients/jobs);

➡ something of why you're particularly keen to work with this kind of organisation or person. Sometimes a little flattery (if it's genuine and it's tastefully done) can be very helpful!

Keep the email as short as possible. The shorter the email, the more likely recipients are to read it. Then send it to everyone you know who you think would be willing to help. Ask them in the email to forward it to anyone else that they think could help.

If you're better on the phone or in person, make use of that too, but the advantage of email is that if you do it well it may go viral, that is, spread far beyond your group of friends and colleagues.

If you've succeeded in creating a following using the kind of strategies described in the previous chapter, also put the word out to your followers that you have something of interest to them.

Myth 15: I can't talk to anyone until I have some fancy business cards printed and my website launched

This is nonsense. It is almost always possible for you to win your first playcheque before you have a website, business cards or much of the other paraphernalia of self-employment. Don't use those things as an excuse. You can always type up a one-page brochure in a word processor and send it by email. Remember that your first sale is likely to be a contact from a friend or colleague so they will hopefully be more forgiving that you're not yet professionally polished. Business cards are overrated anyway. Most cards handed out to people are never looked at again. It's much more important you take someone else's card if you're interested in selling your services or products to them. At least then you're in control of getting in contact.

When you get there, celebrate!

When you win your first playcheque, whether it's selling your first product/artwork/MP3, or winning your first freelance project or contract, pause for a moment and celebrate. You just got paid to play. Don't just brush it off because you're still a long way off making enough to live on. Go celebrate with some friends or with your support team.

Your first experience probably wasn't ideal. It might not be quite what you really want to get paid for; you might not be happy with what you produced or what you got paid; it might have been nerve-wracking or a bit of an anti-climax. That's OK. Just carry on, notice the feedback and how it feels to do it and keep adjusting to aim for the thing that's the most fun and the most rewarding.

In the next chapter you'll find out how to scale up this first experiment to get paid to play full time.

Put it into play

Keys to this secret:

➡ Look for opportunities to be in flow – do what you're good at and enjoy doing.

➡ Run a campaign to win your first paycheque.

➡ When you get there, celebrate!

What you should have now:

➡ a plan for your killer email to win your first paycheque.

Take ten minutes to play:

➡ Using the offer you created in the last chapter, start crafting your killer email to send.

Exclusive extras on ScrewWorkLetsPlay.com

➡ examples of successful campaigns people have run to win their first paycheque.

Secret nine
How to play full time

I never did a day's work in my life. It was all fun.

Thomas Edison

In the previous chapter you saw how to win your very first playcheque. This chapter will show you how to scale this up and move towards getting paid to play full time. To do this you've got to do something good enough to generate word-of-mouth recommendations.

Derek Sivers, musician and entrepreneur, on spreading the word

Derek Sivers was a professional musician when he founded CD Baby, which then went on to become the largest online retailer of independent music. His advice here for musicians is equally relevant to artists, writers or entrepreneurs.

> *When people say 'Hey man, how do I get my music out there?' I say 'Well, what do your friends think of it? And do they like it enough that they have told all of their friends about it?' When friends hear your music they should say 'Oh my God! This is really good. I want to send this to a friend of mine.' And they want to do it for their own sake, not for your sake. That's important. You don't want to have that thing where you're asking friends to help promote you as some kind of favour to you as a friend. They have to want to spread the word the same way that somebody who saw the Mentos and Diet Coke video on YouTube thinks it's hilarious and wants to send it to their friends. It has to be that same impulse.*

The bottom line on scaling up your project is that there has to be excitement on both sides – you're excited by what you're doing but what you're doing is also exciting other people.

What's your next step after winning your first playcheque? It's to do it again and prove your first sale wasn't just a fluke. Find yourself a group of test subjects, or guinea pigs, to repeat the process with. If you can find ten people who love what you're offering so much that they want more of it and they spontaneously rave about it to other people, then you've hit the jackpot. As marketing guru Seth Godin wrote on his blog about this very topic, 'If they love it, they'll each find you ten more people (or a hundred or a thousand or, perhaps, just three). Repeat. If they don't love it, you need a new product. Start over.' Until you can find ten people who are excited by your work, all the marketing tricks in the world won't help you.

There isn't such a great mystery as to who's going to be a success and who isn't. Are you getting clear signals that the world (or at least the little bit of it you are interested in) wants more of what you're offering? If not, take a moment to reflect on what you need to change – are you still doing something that you're not really that keen on? Are you offering something people don't really need (check it solves a problem)? Are you offering it to the wrong people? Or are you enjoying it but you're just not good enough at it yet? If so, stick at it. Consider getting other people in to guide you or to do the bits that you're not so strong at yet. You don't even have to be the person that creates the product or delivers the service. Perhaps your skill is in marketing the idea you've had, or building the systems to support it or doing the deals to win the work. Then collaborate with others to create the product or deliver the work.

You'll know when you've got something good because others will tell you.

The moment Leslie Scott realised her game Jenga was going to be a hit

Early on, I played Jenga with professional sportspeople at a fund-raising event and they loved the game. I woke up the next morning thinking you just show this game to people and they love it and get totally hooked on it and I thought well maybe I should start a business and put the game on the market.

I've since designed and published forty games, none as commercially successful as Jenga but just as fun and exciting to create. Getting something on the market that never existed before is exciting. I wouldn't have done any of this if it hadn't been challenging and fun to do. And when the fun stops, it's time to move on.

Once you've won your first paycheque and repeated the experience with ten people who love what you do, you can start to scale it up. Let's look at the different ways you can get paid to play full time. There is no reason why you should restrict yourself to just one of these. In fact, you are likely to end up with a portfolio career of several strands. The question now is, simply, which one do you want to start with?

The Job 2.0

The conventional job is not a good vehicle for getting paid to play. The problem is that you have to fit into a shape carved out by someone else. It's very difficult to get into flow because it doesn't go down very well in a job if you say, 'I don't like doing that task, so I'm not going to do it'.

The good news is that there is an alternative to the old-fashioned one-size-fits-all job. It's the customised job: Job 2.0, if you will. A customised job is one that you create from scratch or, at least, shape yourself. It's what happens when you come at the world of the job with the player's mindset and ask, 'What do I want to create for myself? What value can I bring?' Here's how to create one: think of what your ideal work would be (based on your thinking so far in your playbook) and run a campaign as shown earlier to go get it. Avoid job adverts, recruitment agencies and HR departments.

Myth 16: I've been applying for jobs and talking to agencies and I've got nowhere, so it must be impossible

It's said that up to 70 per cent of jobs are unadvertised. The rest are filled through personal connections. Jobs filled by this route are often more flexible than ones that are advertised and screened by HR departments. Recruitment agencies rarely help you change career because they are paid to fill vacancies as quickly as possible and will look for the closest match with the greatest experience. Small companies are usually more flexible than large ones. This means that they are likely to be more open to negotiating on what your role will be, what experience you need, and the structure you will work in. If you can impress them enough, you should be able to shape or even create the role you are seeking.

But if the jobs are not advertised, how do you find them? Find ways to hang out with people who are in the industry and particularly those who are in a position to give you work. Remember that if you love this industry or type of work, you should enjoy going to their networking meetings, conferences and events. Get seen. Play the fame game to get noticed. Make it a play project to run an event, or a networking meeting, freelance at an exhibition, write a blog about this world or interview its thought leaders.

Here's how I created the last three customised jobs I had before going self-employed

1. I interviewed at a small software company advertising two jobs I was interested in and I asked that they combine them into one job for me. They agreed.

2. I met someone involved in setting up a new ebusiness consultancy. (I met him at an interview for a different job that I did not get and did not particularly want.) I continued to speak to him for a period of six months as the new company took shape. I suspect he never actually read my CV. He later said, 'I just knew you would be good for the company'. I ended up CTO (Chief Technology Officer) of a division of a very friendly and creative company.

3. A small group of us moved as a team from a small company to a global corporation. In this case, someone with experience of the world of recruitment arranged meetings with several big corporations in our industry. We were eventually hired as a team to start a new service line.

The great thing about this process is that when you deliberately seek out your ideal job, your enthusiasm shines through in the hiring process. Now imagine the tables were turned and you were in a position to hire someone. Wouldn't you be more interested in someone who had sought you out especially and explained why they were keen to work for your organisation in particular?

The customised job rarely gives you quite the same flexibility as self-employment to sculpt your working life exactly how you want it. The advantage, however, is that you don't have to worry about marketing yourself. If your final destination is still self-employment, the customised job can be a good stepping stone on your way out of the job market. A part-time customised job can also be a useful part of a portfolio career. It often provides more of a team experience than self-employment does. And if you really have terrible self-discipline, a boss is a useful thing!

Going freestyle

The miserable history of work is represented by the uninspired vocabulary we have to describe it. We need a new word for the kind of lives we are creating now. 'Self-employed' is something found on a tax form, business man/woman brings an image of a middle-aged person in a conservative suit talking about ROIs and KPIs. 'Entrepreneur' is a word beginners have a problem identifying with.

None of these words explain the whole reason for leaving the world of jobs – freedom, individuality, fun, the chance to finally create something only you can create. Author Barbara Winter calls us 'Joyfully Jobless'; Daniel Pink calls us the 'Free Agent Nation'. I think of it as going freestyle.

Whatever we call it, if you haven't tried it yet, it can seem like a huge leap and you might be labouring under the popular myths surrounding it. Here are three of the most common.

Myth 17: It's safer to have a job than to be self-employed

If you're still in a job right now, you might find your colleagues warning how much safer it is to stay in a job. But in fact, as an employee, you can be fired or made redundant at any time with as little as a month's notice and little or no redundancy pay. A job is actually rather like being self-employed but with only one client: your boss. When you're self-employed you will have several or even hundreds of clients. You're very unlikely to get fired by all your clients at the same time. The risky bit is starting a business without testing and winning some clients first, which we've already seen how to avoid.

Myth 18: I'd be crazy to go self-employed in the current economic climate

When the economy's on a downturn, it certainly makes sense to test out your ideas before you jump from your current employment. However, don't assume that you should give up on self-employment altogether. People still make money in a downturn; in fact some businesses do better. If you can save people money by providing something they need in a cheaper way, you could even get rich. The supermarkets that are perceived as cheapest experienced a boom in the most recent downturn.

On the flipside, the richest consumers tend to be insulated from fluctuations in the economy so it might be the right time to move up market and offer something to the most affluent in society. Learn from the wisest people in your field and watch what they do.

Myth 19: I need an original idea to start a business

This is the myth of the great invention; why is it as soon as we start a business we imagine we must invent a new kind of vacuum cleaner or a completely original concept for a restaurant? Programmes like *Dragons' Den* promote this idea. If you are actually an inventor and have been playing with inventions for as long as you can remember, keep inventing. For the rest of us, just take a look down your local high street. How many hairdressers are there? How many pubs are there? How many newsagents? You don't need a new idea no one's thought of before to go into business: you just need to do something well, make a profit, and play the fame game intelligently.

We're lucky. Even ten years ago, the options for starting your own business were far smaller and the risks much higher. Thanks to the internet, now anyone can launch a business in a day. There are kinds of businesses you can launch that a decade ago didn't even exist. What this means is that you no longer have to mortgage your house to start something. You don't even need to leave your job. You don't need to rent a shop on the high street and spend tens of thousands fitting it out. You can go online and build a shop in an afternoon – for free. Whatever grand vision you might have for your work, there is a way to start right now, in a scaled-down form, test it out, then scale it up. And there is no reason to restrict yourself to just one money-making activity.

Create your portfolio career

If you get bored easily doing just one thing, like the Scanner personality we talked about earlier, you can build a portfolio career to keep you interested. There's no reason to pretend you will one day become ruthlessly focused. Instead, deliberately build a working life that has lots of variety in it. Build a portfolio of multiple income streams. Some might be selling your time, others could be running teleclasses, affiliate marketing, or even property investment. If you want to have multiple income streams, make sure some of them are low-maintenance income as described in Secret seven. Once you've set them up, they will then continue to pay you while you start something else.

Some income streams might only make you a few hundred pounds a month. But each one you add will take you closer to your desired target while giving your plenty of variety in your work. Having more than one string to your bow can actually be safer than relying on one line of work. If the market changes suddenly, some of your income streams may suffer, others may be relatively unaffected or even boosted.

A portfolio career is not always easy to manage. The best way to make it work is to be clear which of your income streams is your cash cow and make sure you don't let it slip no matter how busy you are with other things. Even if you eventually intend to have multiple projects running concurrently, only launch one at a time. Projects require the most energy and attention when they are first launched. Get something working to a point where it doesn't need your constant attention before thinking of launching another project.

Remember that most projects you want to succeed require you to both create something and market it. If the projects are very different and aimed at different types of people, you're going to have to put a lot of time and effort in. It is far easier if there is a common strand to what you do. Get known for something: be 'the internet ideas guy', 'the builder that actually turns up', 'the coder that can communicate', 'the friendly techie'. If you can find that theme that captures your real talent, it becomes much easier for people to understand what you do and so recommend you to other people. A good way to look at it is to do several things for the same market of people or companies. That way, once you have become well known among internet start-ups, or women entrepreneurs over 40, or people who love to travel independently, you can easily offer them the other things you do. For example, if you get known for being a virtual assistant to busy consultants, and you then learn how to set up simple websites, you can offer your clients a special service to create their first consultancy website.

Collaborate for speed

A good way to make a large project happen quickly or to be involved in multiple projects is to collaborate with others and focus on the part you are best at (and enjoy).

Myth 20: I can't go self-employed because I'm no good at selling/marketing/IT/finances/creative ideas

You don't need to know or do everything in your business. Find other people to do the bits you're not so good at. If you love presenting but hate finance, collaborate with someone who loves spreadsheets but hates performing in front of an audience. You don't even need your own idea to start a business: you can team up with someone else who's got the good idea and bring your people skills, technical skills, sales skills or organisation skills.

A lot of people make the mistake of collaborating with people who are too similar – you're both very extravert and big-picture oriented, or you've both introverted geeks. This leaves big holes in your capabilities. If you're both geeks, who's going to do the sales and marketing? If you're both loaded with ideas, who's going to turn them into a plan and a timeline you can follow?

To be really successful you will need to collaborate with very different personalities. As entrepreneur and business coach Judith Morgan says, 'You have to work with people who irritate you'. As an introvert you might find the sales guy kind of showy and over the top, and he might find you a bit dull and serious. As long as there's enough mutual respect, it could be a good combination. Think back to Wealth Dynamics in Secret two; look at the descriptions of the profiles and notice where you are weakest. Collaborate with someone who can fill those holes for you.

The other great benefit of collaboration is to win business quickly. If you know you've got something good to offer but you just can't get customers fast enough, here's a great trick: get other people to market you. You know the problem you solve and who you solve it for. Now ask yourself, where do these people hang out? What do they read? What magazines do they buy? What events do they attend? Whose other products do they buy? Once you know, work out how you can put yourself in front of these people. Can you write an article for a website or a magazine that you know your ideal client will be reading? Or give a talk to an audience of just the right kind of people? Or ask someone with an email database of thousands of the right people to mention your new product? You can offer to do the same in return or pay them a commission on the sales you make. This way you don't need to build your own market from scratch by collecting piles of business cards at endless networking events. Borrow someone else's market.

Do the numbers work?

Before you go much further, let's check that the numbers add up.

Myth 21: I need a 30-page business plan before I can start

In the early stages of getting paid to play, you really don't need a formal business plan. It is, however, a very good idea to do a back-of-an-envelope calculation for your own benefit. I call this 'The 3-line business plan'.

Here's the version of the 3-line business plan if you're selling a service. Think about your desired monthly income. Then estimate what you think the average client or project will pay you. Divide your desired income by this number and you know how many clients/projects you need per month. Now check, can you actually handle this number of clients in a month? Remember that it takes time to find clients and you also need to put aside time for training, administration and so on.

If you're selling physical products, work out your profit on each product and then calculate how many you will have to sell to make your desired income. You can quickly come to appreciate why finding someone to sell your products in bulk is very important!

If you're selling information products, your income will equal the number of website visitors times the percentage of visitors who buy times the price of the product (less any commission or payment processing fees). Just realise that your percentage of buyers might be 1 per cent or less! Don't forget that there will probably be multiple income streams to factor into these calculations.

Since you might need to live on less while you're getting set up, it's important to know what the minimum income is that covers your basic expenses without the frills. Then know what a comfortable income is that you could sustain for longer and also work out what your desired income is. You might be surprised how few people do these simple sums. They're important to look at because they'll affect your choice of business. If you need £100,000 to survive, you might need to rule out some options you would consider if you only needed £25,000 a year.

When to quit your day job

Don't be too quick to jump from the work that's currently providing your income: better to gain momentum first while still being paid elsewhere. Being stressed about money is not a state conducive to playfulness.

Once you know that the numbers work, you've proved that people want what you're offering and you have more demand than you can service in your spare time, you may well be ready to jump.

Innocent Drinks

Innocent Drinks is a British company founded by three college friends in 1999 to create natural fruit smoothies. The company now has a 71 per cent share of the £169 million UK smoothie market but started with nothing more than a stall at a music festival, as the founders explain:

> In the summer of 1998 when we had developed our first smoothie recipes but were still nervous about giving up our proper jobs, we bought £500 worth of fruit, turned it into smoothies and sold them from a stall at a little music festival in London. We put up a big sign saying 'Do you think we should give up our jobs to make these smoothies?' and put out a bin saying 'YES' and a bin saying 'NO' and asked people to put the empty bottle in the right bin. At the end of the weekend the 'YES' bin was full so we went in the next day and resigned.

Innocent had spent six months creating and testing smoothie recipes before they turned up at the music festival. They sold 24 smoothies on their first day in business. Today, ten years on, they sell two million a week.

Taking redundancy can help you make your escape. If a redundancy programme has begun where you work (or there are rumours of one), be clear on your position: do you want to leave or not? Don't just wait and see what happens. Make up your mind, then see if you can manoeuvre yourself into or out of the firing line accordingly.

Once redundancy is offered, remember that the terms can be negotiable even when it doesn't look like it. Always ask if you want to modify your leaving date a bit or keep a benefit like a company car for a while. You'd be surprised how often you can get this. You may think you have nothing in your hand to negotiate with, but most companies want to part on good terms so will be open to sweetening the process if they can. If redundancies aren't on offer, it may still be possible to negotiate favourable terms for your departure such as paid 'gardening leave'.

How long is all this going to take?

Here's the bad news. Malcolm Gladwell among others has made the argument that it takes 10,000 hours, or approximately six years full time, to become a world-class success in any field, whether it's rock music, public speaking, writing, or programming. This is why if you're switching fields completely, you can expect it to take a while to get established in the new thing.

Here's the good news. If what you're doing is fun much of the time, then six years go by pretty quickly.

Here's the even better news. You're already a world-class expert. At what? You're an expert at being you. No one does *you* better. You've spent your whole life doing it and you get good at what you do a lot. Whatever your moment of magic is, you've been doing it since you were a young child; talking to people, making people laugh, cheering people up, reading and writing, drawing, studying, organising, negotiating, savouring food, enjoying nature, patching relationships up. All this practice has built circuits in your brain that others just don't have. You see the world differently. If you've been performing and telling jokes to friends and family as long as you can remember, but you've never done any formal public speaking then you need to learn the practical skills like timing, story structure and so on. But you're not starting from scratch. If you love doing something, you're almost certainly already doing it somewhere in your life even if you don't recognise it.

Focus on mining these natural talents, develop your skills around them, and look out for a common theme in everything you do that you can really commit to. The theme might be a certain kind of person or segment of the market that you help; it might be one thing you are known for doing well (as we saw earlier in portfolio careers); it could be an overarching problem you are set on addressing (from Secret five), or it might be a brand you have created. When you find your theme and really commit to it, people sense it and you start to attract the opportunities and income you want. It might even make you rich, as we'll see in the next chapter.

Put it into play

Keys to this secret:

➡ Run your offer again with a group of ten test subjects.

➡ Are people raving about you yet? If not, keep adjusting until they do.

➡ Decide your route to playing full time: the customised job or freestyle career.

➡ Collaborate with others for speed and to enable you to manage a portfolio of projects.

➡ Check the numbers work before you go any further.

What you should have now:

➡ a strategy for scaling up your first test-run to something that could work as a full-time living.

Take ten minutes to play:

➡ Allow yourself to daydream a little about the point when you are getting paid to play full time. Describe what your portfolio of work looks like in your playbook.

➡ Brainstorm ways you can collaborate with other people to make this daydream come true a little faster.

Exclusive extras on ScrewWorkLetsPlay.com

➡ Listen to audio recordings of my interview with Derek Sivers, the founder of CD Baby and Leslie Scott, creator of Jenga.

Secret ten

How to play your way to the rich life

You can get everything in life you want if you will just help enough other people to get what they want.

Zig Ziglar, American author and speaker

In the previous chapter we saw how to scale up what you offer to get paid to play full time. So is it possible to get *rich* from playing? This chapter will help you work out what rich actually means to you and get you a little closer to it sooner than you might think.

There are plenty of players that have turned their experimental projects into million-selling businesses. Derek Sivers turned fiddling around on the web to sell his own music into a business that made over $100 million in sales. Leslie Scott turned a game using her baby brother's wooden blocks into one of the world's best-selling games. Mike Southon is a serial entrepreneur of 17 start-ups, now a mentor for other entrepreneurs, and delivers over a hundred presentations every year, all over the world. And despite the long hours he says 'it doesn't feel like work at all, it's all play'.

The principle here is to create wealth from providing genuine value to the world. When you have proven that you can do that in a repeatable way as shown in the preceding chapters, the challenge then becomes how to scale up to provide more value to more people.

If you think getting rich is all about profit at any cost, you're choosing the wrong role models. When your wealth is based on providing real value, everybody wins. Getting richer goes hand in hand with extending the positive impact you are having. As Google CEO Eric Schmidt recently told *New Yorker* writer Ken Auletta,

'The goal of the company is not to monetize anything, the goal is to change the world – and monetization is a technique to do that.'

Players are driven by what they want to create as much as anything else. As Anita Roddick, founder of the Body Shop, once said, 'Entrepreneurs want to create a livelihood from an idea that has obsessed them. Money will grease the wheels, but becoming a millionaire is not the aim of the true entrepreneur. In fact, most entrepreneurs I know don't give a damn about the accumulation of money. What gets their juices going is seeing how far an idea can go.' Ironically it's exactly this attitude that often leads to the greatest financial rewards. As Apple CEO Steve Jobs once said, 'I was worth about over a million dollars when I was twenty-three and over ten million dollars when I was twenty-four, and over a hundred million dollars when I was twenty-five and it wasn't that important because I never did it for the money.'

Creating real wealth from your play takes plenty of time and effort but if you master the following five keys, you should make the journey a little smoother and a little shorter.

1. Create your vision of the rich life

What does 'rich' actually mean to you? You might be thinking of a certain amount of money but in fact isn't it really about experiencing a different kind of lifestyle, a rich life? Think about what your rich life would look like. What would be different for you? What would you own? What are the experiences you would like wealth to provide for you? Write it down in your playbook and find images to represent it. Putting your focus on the experience rather than a number allows you to find creative ways to get what you want sooner. If you want to have a mansion in France, you might find a way to have at least some of that experience very soon without becoming a millionaire. Perhaps you could find someone who's willing to rent out a house to you in exchange for decorating it, or you could rent the house to run a workshop or conference in and so have other people pay you to be there.

Don't put off your happiness until you reach your financial goals. Savour moments in your life that represent what you want more of. Recently I found myself having lunch with a friend outside a Thai restaurant in the London sunshine. As we sipped lemongrass tea and discussed her imminent move to America to further her acting, the conversation turned to money and doing what you love. I said that I was feeling rich right then – because if I had a million pounds in the bank, I wouldn't choose to be doing anything different. I'd still be sitting with some good company eating tasty Thai food in the sunshine. So you could say that I am already rich (and the whole experience only cost us £15 each).

Catch yourself feeling rich. Notice those moments when there is nothing else you need, nowhere else you should be, and no one else you would rather be with because in that moment, you too are already rich.

If you can't enjoy what you have, you can't enjoy more of it.

Richard Bandler, co-creator of Neuro-Linguistic Programming (NLP)

If you can't appreciate the rich moments you are having right now, you might discover you won't be able to appreciate it if and when you really do achieve your financial dreams. We've all seen the millionaires who just can't stop; however much money they get, whatever they buy, they're never satisfied. That's not happiness.

And of course the other reason to appreciate how rich you already are is because it tends to attract more of the same, which means you'll realise those financial dreams all the sooner. People like to hang out with happy people and they like to hire those who look like they're thriving. In fact the less you look like you need the work and the less available you appear to be, the more people want you – they assume you must be good!

Is your rich life about the freedom to travel?

Would you like to live somewhere sunnier or be free to travel anywhere in the world? Why not start now? Since it's now possible to run a business with nothing more than a phone, a laptop, and an internet connection, do you really need to stay in the country? How would you like to travel the world and still make a living? Join the new tribe of location-independent entrepreneurs who travel the world while running their businesses from a laptop.

Have laptop, will travel

Chris Guillebeau is a world traveller and professional blogger. He makes a full-time living from his blog The Art of Non-Conformity while travelling the world on his mission to visit every country on Earth. He's not wildly financially rich (yet) but he's created a life most only ever dream of.

He's recognised as an expert on cheap air travel, 'I sometimes fly First Class before checking into a $15 hostel – kind of ironic, but it's fun.' And he's often to be found with his laptop far off the tourist track: 'I really enjoyed being the only westerner in a bush taxi last month from Mozambique to Swaziland.'

This is business as usual for Chris: 'The thing is that a lot of what I do is the same wherever I go, and personally I like that – I write, meet people, drink coffee, have fun. Hopefully every day has moments like that – whether in Bhutan, where I'm going next, in Kuwait, where I just came from, or while working at home in Oregon.'

Look at chrisguillebeau.com and Lea Woodward's location-independent.com to find tips on how to get paid while travelling the world.

Is your rich life about free time?

Tom Hodgkinson is editor of bi-annual magazine *The Idler* and is author of several books including *How to be Idle* and *How to be Free*. I interviewed him about the working life he has created and he explained that he works from 9 a.m. to 1 p.m., concentrating on writing, then checks his emails before taking the rest of the afternoon off. He's free then to have lunch, read, take a nap, go for a walk, play his ukelele, or do some gardening. Instead of working relentlessly to get rich, Tom is happy to settle on a medium-level income and advocates thrift, 'cutting out any expense you don't really need. Your children will think you're really mean but you'll end up having more time to play cards with them.'

If your vision of a rich life is about plenty of free time and relaxation rather than yachts and mansions, you can choose to structure your life accordingly. And when you start really enjoying your day-to-day life, you might find you no longer need to spend so much money on the things you used to buy to compensate for being miserable at work. When I added it up, I was shocked to realise that when I was working in a corporation, I was spending several hundred pounds a year on cappuccinos – just to get me through the day.

Is your rich life about the power to change the world?

If so, the model for you may be to create a social enterprise: an organisation that applies commercial strategies to achieve a social or environmental purpose. The power of this model is financial sustainability; rather than relying on a continual campaign for more donations or government funding, the enterprise generates profits that can be reinvested to further your mission. The same rules apply that you must generate genuine value and find a way to monetise it. Then the more you grow the enterprise, the more positive impact you can have.

2. Manage your money like a millionaire

A client going through career change once said to me, 'I wish I could just have a million pounds sitting in my account so I didn't have to think about money any more'. The problem is that even if you had a million pounds, if you spent a million and a half you'd still be broke (as many lottery winners have found out). There is never a point when you don't have to think about money and manage it well. Learn the habit now. You're unlikely to reach that million without it. There are now some excellent books and courses that make the whole topic, believe it or not, fun!

Start your play fund

One good discipline is to split your income and allocate it to different accounts for different purposes. Put aside a percentage for long-term saving. You might also choose to give 5–10 per cent to a charity or cause of your choice. You then have the pleasure of knowing that as your income increases, so does your contribution. And don't forget money for fun. Put aside 10 per cent for your play fund. This is a savings fund for your play project and for anything else that feels fun and playful. Use your play fund to save up for a significant purchase for your play project: a good quality photo printer, a music software package, or a course to further your latest interest. Also use your play fund to treat yourself occasionally: pay for a fancy night out or other treat whenever you hit a release date for a project. It's a kind thing to do for yourself and primes your subconscious to know there is a payoff when you've gone all out to get a project done.

When I had my first article published in a national newspaper, I took the whole payment out of the bank as cash and blew it on what was then the very latest portable music player. It seemed extravagant at the time but I ended up carrying it with me everywhere. And every time I looked at it, I remembered that it was my own creativity and initiative that had paid for it.

Is all this talk of spending money on indulging yourself pressing your buttons yet? Good. Read on.

3. Remove your internal blocks to getting rich

Have you noticed how some people always seem to have money throughout their lives and other people with similar talents and opportunities are always broke? Where are you on this scale? What's your pattern? Have you always struggled? Or always managed to just get by? Or have you usually done well for yourself?

If money has often been a problem for you, or if you're doing OK but can't see how to do much better, it may be because you have some negative beliefs about money and what it would mean to be rich. If you think selling is tacky, marketing is conning people, rich people are all selfish, or charging a good price is ripping people off, it will be very difficult to get paid well for what you do.

I worked with a client once who had never earned very much money despite having a lot of talent, some great ideas and a certain level of fame. Sitting in my garden, I asked her, 'What do you think of rich people?' She burst out laughing and had to admit she immediately thought of all the worst possible icons of wealth: the selfish cigar-smoking tycoon, the entrepreneur that tramples on everyone else to get ahead. The problem with this is that it's very difficult to become something you despise. I asked her instead to think of three financially successful people that she actually respected. It took her a while but she came up with three great role models. I set her the homework to find images of these people on the web, print them out and place them somewhere she'll see them when she's working. This is a great exercise for anyone to do. Who would your three people be? Think of them as your virtual mentors.

Our beliefs and habits around money have a huge amount of influence on where we sit on the financial scale. If you pride yourself on not being concerned about money, you probably won't have any. Remember that money makes play sustainable; there are no prizes for being a starving artist or entrepreneur. If you feel comfortable earning a modest income and then start to earn more, you might subconsciously sabotage yourself to bring yourself back to what feels normal. And what feels normal is strongly influenced by your social group.

You are the average of the five people you spend the most time with.

Jim Rohn, American entrepreneur, author and speaker

Here's a little experiment. Add up the income of the five people you spend the most time with. Divide it by five to get the average. It's typical to find that your income is pretty close to this number. We saw in Secret four 'How to guarantee your success' how we are hypnotised by the thoughts, habits and beliefs we are surrounded by every day so it's not surprising that our closest friends will have an influence on our mindset and our expectations of life.

Imagine you spend all your time with people who earn half what you do. Your current income might start to feel pretty rich. In fact you might begin to feel a bit uncomfortable around your friends, even a little guilty. Now imagine you are transported to another social circle where you spend all your time with people who earn at least twice what you currently do. You might start to feel a little embarrassed about your income and start to wonder if you could use some of the techniques your peers have used to get where they are. Can you see how these two very different experiences might influence your financial expectations and even your actions regarding money?

People who have created unusual levels of wealth of their own have different strategies and habits from ours; these are bound to rub off on you over time. If you are serious about getting paid to play – and paid well – think about augmenting your social circle with some people who share your new values and might encourage some different approaches to wealth.

4. Dare to charge what you're worth

It's impossible to get rich if you're not willing to charge well for (or otherwise monetise) the value you provide. Negotiating compensation for your work can be challenging, particularly if what you're selling is your own expertise or your artistic output. If you have a habit of undercharging for what you do, take a tip from Pablo Picasso.

A Picasso original

According to the story, some decades ago a woman was strolling along a street in Paris when she spotted Picasso sketching at a sidewalk café.

The woman asked Picasso if he would sketch her, and charge her accordingly. Picasso agreed.

In just a few minutes, she had an original Picasso sketch of herself.

'And what do I owe you?' she asked.

'Five thousand francs', he answered.

'But it only took you 3 minutes!' she said.

'No,' Picasso said, 'It took all my life.'

Remember that our value to others is based on all that we bring – our natural talents, the skills we have developed and the experiences we have sought out. Think of everything you have invested in yourself and your business. Take out your playbook and add it all up – the training, the workshops, the costs of setting up your business. Include anything that you know you draw upon in your work. This is not just formal training; if your round-the-world trip taught you a heap of stuff about people, budgeting and organisation, put it on the list. Add a figure for all the years you lived on less than you would have liked because you were building something new. Now, does what you're currently charging reflect this value? If not, start to think how you can charge according to the value you provide, not just the time you put in. You might find you attract better clients or customers; undervaluing yourself tends to attract clients who undervalue you. Being too cheap sometimes puts good people off you altogether.

Would you like to get rich quick?

To get paid to play, you need to know how to play with capitalism. Capitalism may have its problems but for the time being it's here to stay so you might as well make friends with it. Interacting with your market is part of the game of being a player.

One of the fundamental models that underpins a free market is that of 'supply and demand'. I'm sure you've heard of it and yet many of us seem to forget all about it when it comes to earning a living off our own back.

What it means for you is that two things contribute to making more money from your playing: a smaller number of people who can supply what you do, or a larger number of people with a demand for it. Choosing your projects to increase either side of this equation will bring you a better return: provide something in short supply and choose things in great or rising demand.

Supply and demand also explains why there is no real way to get rich quickly. If there were an easy way to do something valuable and make you money, lots of people would rush to do it. Once that happened, the product would no longer be valuable because there would be an oversupply. When it was first realised that you could make money by putting adverts on Google for other people's products and getting paid commission, many people rushed to do it. As a result, the price for the ads went up, the market was flooded and it became much more difficult to make money. It is still possible (I do it) but it takes time to develop the skill to rise above the competition.

The exception to this rule is that there are occasionally critical moments in every industry when opportunities open up. Regulation changes, new technology appears or a market reaches a tipping point. If you are ready to seize these moments when they appear, you can make money very quickly. To take advantage early before the bandwagon begins, you need to already be operating in that area and have the expertise to recognise the opportunity and make use of it. By the time you see someone writing a book or running a workshop on how to make a quick buck from a new opportunity, you can be sure that the market will be far more competitive. That doesn't mean you shouldn't go near it. If getting into this area would be fun for you, your enthusiasm should support you in developing the skills you'll need to stand out from the 'me toos'. And whenever you're out there playing with a project, always keep an eye open for the moments when good opportunities appear.

How to get (a little more) rich quick

There may be no easy formula to become a millionaire overnight, but there are some simple ways to make yourself a little richer right away. Charge more for what you do by following my P.R.I.C.E. strategy. Some of my clients have more than doubled their prices using this system.

P is for Product

Sell the right thing. The right thing is what there is great demand for, particularly something that solves a significant problem for people. Generally speaking, the bigger the problem you solve and the more people that have it, the more money you can make. You can also quickly increase what you typically make from each customer by bundling products and services into a package.

If you have specialist skills you enjoy using, this can help tip supply and demand in your favour. Invest in getting really good at what you do. When you find something you enjoy doing and have good skills for, don't be afraid to specialise in it. Then it's easier for people to understand what you offer and spread the word. Imagine you had lower back pain: who would you try first, a normal osteopath or a specialist 'Lower Back Pain Clinic' if there were such a thing near you?

R is for the Right people

You can have the best product in the world but if the market you're approaching can't afford it, you won't make much money. Corporations, for example, can afford to pay much more than the general public for what you offer because what you do might benefit many staff or customers and the cost is spread across the whole business. If what you're offering is too expensive for your ideal client, find a different way to deliver it that makes it cheaper but allows you to provide it to more people. Can you provide some of your value over the internet using the strategies in Secret seven?

I is for Increasing trust

It's much easier to sell what you offer if you can build trust and reduce the perceived risk for the buyer. Focus on creating a good track record and communicate it by encouraging word of mouth and using what's referred to as 'social proof' such as testimonials and case studies.

A guarantee can dramatically reduce the perceived risk for your buyers. Offering a no-questions-asked, money-back guarantee on your product or service often makes far more in additional sales than what you might lose from the odd person taking advantage of it.

C is for Communicating value

Learn how to effectively communicate the value of what you do and stand by it. Don't apologise for charging a high price. Draw people in by identifying the problem you solve, then explain the benefits they will get and how much better their situation will be after they have used you or your product. If you're selling your expertise, price yourself on results not on time. I once charged over a thousand pounds for a one-hour phone call and had no complaints because I was sharing my specialist expertise on a critical decision.

E is for Expect it and ask for it!

The biggest reason I have managed to get paid so well for many of the things I have done, whether it's doubling my contract rate or getting £1,300 for my first magazine article, is that I simply dared to ask. It helps here to be clear on why you want it and deserve it. If you're worried you'll lose customers by putting up prices, try the new higher price on a special product or just on new customers. If you're good, you might be surprised just what people are willing to pay. And if it encourages you to raise the quality of your work even further, that's no bad thing.

If you're worried you'll price yourself out of your market, look for someone else that is charging a good price in your field. How do they do it? What can you use from them? Often the answer is to redefine yourself so that you are no longer compared with lower-priced competitors. If you're a web designer that also knows a lot about branding, relaunch as a brand designer and shake off the run-of-the-mill web design competition.

What to do when someone says 'I can't afford it'

You may find this hard to believe but it's never about the money. If someone says 'I can't afford it' what they mean is 'I can't see the value yet'. As long as you're selling to the right person then you simply haven't communicated the value well enough yet.

Would you have paid £5,000 for this book? Probably not. What if the book was the only copy specially written by Richard Branson and contained his secret guaranteed formula to make you a millionaire in 12 months? Perhaps you would – even if you had to sell your car to get it! It's not the price that's the problem.

Ultimately, if you've effectively communicated how you can solve someone's problem and they're still not going to buy, there is nothing you can do. Just move on to the next person. Some people will never spend the extra for good quality.

5. Choose a rich strategy

Remember, the best way to make a living is to provide genuine value to the world. If you're doing this then getting rich will mean providing more value to more people. If you want to make a million you have to provide a million of value. When you get there, you will have benefited others as much as yourself. I get annoyed when I see people providing great value to a tiny number of people but failing to ever expand their reach. They have never created a strategy to scale up or have never dared to play the fame game and get noticed. This is everyone's loss.

As we've seen earlier, it's difficult to get really rich selling your time or making your own handmade products: there are only so many hours in the day. Ultimately you need something that can scale beyond what you can do on your own. You need a business. Your role then moves from working in delivering the product or service to working *on* your business.

To get really rich, solve hard problems. That's what Google did – they entered a crowded marketplace and produced a far superior version of a search engine. Now as Microsoft snap at their heels with their Bing search engine, Google are interested in an even harder problem – they are looking at the real meaning in information so that one day soon you will be able to ask Google 'What should I do today?'

What difficult problem do you feel strongly about and would enjoy playing with? What might engage your interest long enough to make a real impact on it? Making a success of it is likely to take you some considerable time and effort, so choosing something that you'll enjoy along the way is essential.

If you're already doing well in your current business ask yourself, 'How can I provide this value to a lot more people?' Is there a way you can take what you provide personally and make it available to many more people on the internet, or by training others in your techniques, or by doing a deal with a larger company?

Sophie Boss of Beyond Chocolate grew her business with 'Chocolate Fairies'

My sister Audrey and I were running small scale courses and doing everything ourselves. Today we have 15 licensees who run Beyond Chocolate courses all over the UK. We wrote a book which generated far more demand than we could meet with courses, so we launched an online course and two new ebooks. I had always said, 'You can't do this online. Absolutely not. It's got to be personal. How can you possibly offer women the support they need through that medium?' But we found a way to do it that works! – by training what we call Chocolate Fairies who are on the other end of the computer and respond to emails personally within 48 hours. Now we are looking for funding so that we can continue to grow.

Collaborate with others to help you scale. Once you can offer something people really want without having to deliver it yourself, look for connections with others that can quickly multiply your business. Just one good retailer or agent or marketer can transform the money you're making by supplying what you do to a whole new market. And if you follow the process laid out so far in the book they might come and find you before you even go looking!

Start crafting your rich strategy today. Learn from the stories of others in your field to find out how they scaled up to create a business out of their first experiments. If you're determined enough, you can join them in playing your way to your own version of the rich life.

Put it into play

Keys to this secret:

➡ Describe your vision of the rich life and be creative about how you can get some of the experience now.

➡ Manage your money like a millionaire and start your play fund.

➡ Work on your internal blocks to getting rich.

➡ Use the P.R.I.C.E. strategy to charge what you're worth.

➡ Create a rich strategy with something that scales.

What you should have now:

➡ a strategy to maximise the return on your playing and enjoy the process.

Take ten minutes to play:

➡ Set up an account for your play fund.

➡ Brainstorm a way to have a small experience of your rich life now.

➡ Sketch out some ways to create your rich strategy in your playbook.

Exclusive extras on ScrewWorkLetsPlay.com

→ Listen to interviews with successful entrepreneurs including Mike Southon, Leslie Scott (creator of Jenga) and Derek Sivers.

→ Access links to up-to-date resources to learn more about managing money, creating a portable business to support your travels, and workshops on the mindset of wealth.

Let's play

Let's make this really clear; you can always have the experience you really want in your work as long as you're flexible about the form it will come in. You can start right now, and you are *guaranteed* to get it if you simply *do not stop*.

As long as you're in the wrong work or failing to make the most of your talents, you're short-changing not just yourself but the world. As I said to a client recently who was stuck prevaricating about what to do next, 'You know, it's not all about you. Stop obsessing about what to do and whether you can do it and just start doing it – 'cos I'd like to see some of these interesting ideas of yours actually happen.'

We're waiting for you to do your thing. If you haven't take action yet, it's time to start. Pick a play project that will last three to four weeks and take you one step closer to getting paid to do what you love. Grab your playbook (or the nearest scrap of paper), write a list of five things that will get you started. Each should take no more than half an hour, maybe less. Choose one you can do right now. Put the book down. Go do it. Notice the results you get and tune your direction accordingly. Choose your next task and put an appointment in your diary to do that. Repeat. Don't stop.

Let's play. I believe it's your turn.

Bonus content on ScrewWork LetsPlay.com

The accompanying website for this book contains a whole heap of exclusive additional content to help you get paid to play:

➡ Read and listen to full interviews with ten successful players, from people just starting out to millionaires.

➡ More information and website links for every topic covered in each chapter of the book.

➡ Connect with a global online community of players.

➡ More information for Scanners and details of monthly meetings.

➡ Download editable worksheets for you to choose what to do next.

➡ How to access expert coaches for some one-to-one help on choosing what to do next and make a success of it.

➡ More information on Wealth Dynamics and how to take the test.

➡ More on your top dog and how to tame it.

➡ Listen to an audio recording that goes deeper into the topic of identifying problems to solve.

➡ More about blogs, social media and email marketing: which services to use, how to sign up for them and how to use them.

➡ More on how to generate passive income and create information products.

➡ Examples of successful campaigns people have run to win their first playcheque.

➡ Links to some of the best blogs on the web.

- ➡ Links to up-to-date resources to learn more about managing money, creating a portable business to support your travels, and workshops on the mindset of wealth.
- ➡ Details of how to contact me via email and Twitter.

Go to ScrewWorkLetsPlay.com now and dive in.

About War Child UK

Ten per cent of ongoing author royalties for this book will be donated to War Child UK, the international charity that protects children living in the world's most dangerous war zones including Iraq, Afghanistan, Democratic Republic of Congo, and Uganda.

War Child protects children from the brutal effects of war and its consequences. Their work with former child soldiers, children in prison, and children living and working on the streets gives them support, protection and opportunities.

War Child staff are on the ground helping thousands of kids to rebuild their lives. By working with local partners, they provide a number of services for children including:

→ rebuilding schools destroyed by war and getting children back into education;
→ separating children from adult detainees in prison and providing legal aid;
→ reintegrating child soldiers with their families;
→ getting children off the streets after war has forced them to leave home;
→ counselling to help children cope with the effects of war;
→ vocational and professional training which gives them future opportunities;
→ ensuring children get access to food.

War Child makes creative use of music in their work – both to raise funds with their superb cover albums featuring famous names, and in their work with the children themselves. In Bosnia, music therapy was one of the tools to help kids come to terms with their traumatic experiences. And in Kinshasa in the Democratic Republic of Congo, War Child hosted a rap battle for the street kids they work with. They also took some of them into a studio with a Congolese rap artist to record a track about their lives and their dreams for the future.

To read more about War Child, buy their excellent cover albums, or to make a donation, go to www.warchild.org.uk

The 21 myths of work

Index